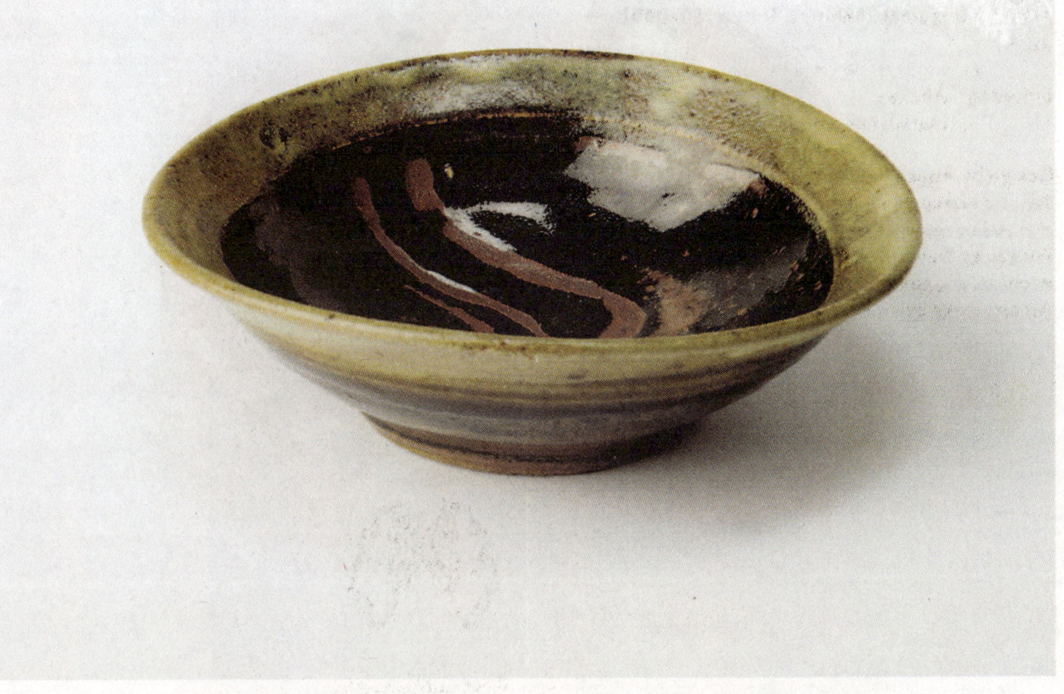

Shoji Hamada
Untitled, c. 1950
Ceramic bowl
2 x 7.5 inches
4.4 x 19.1 cm

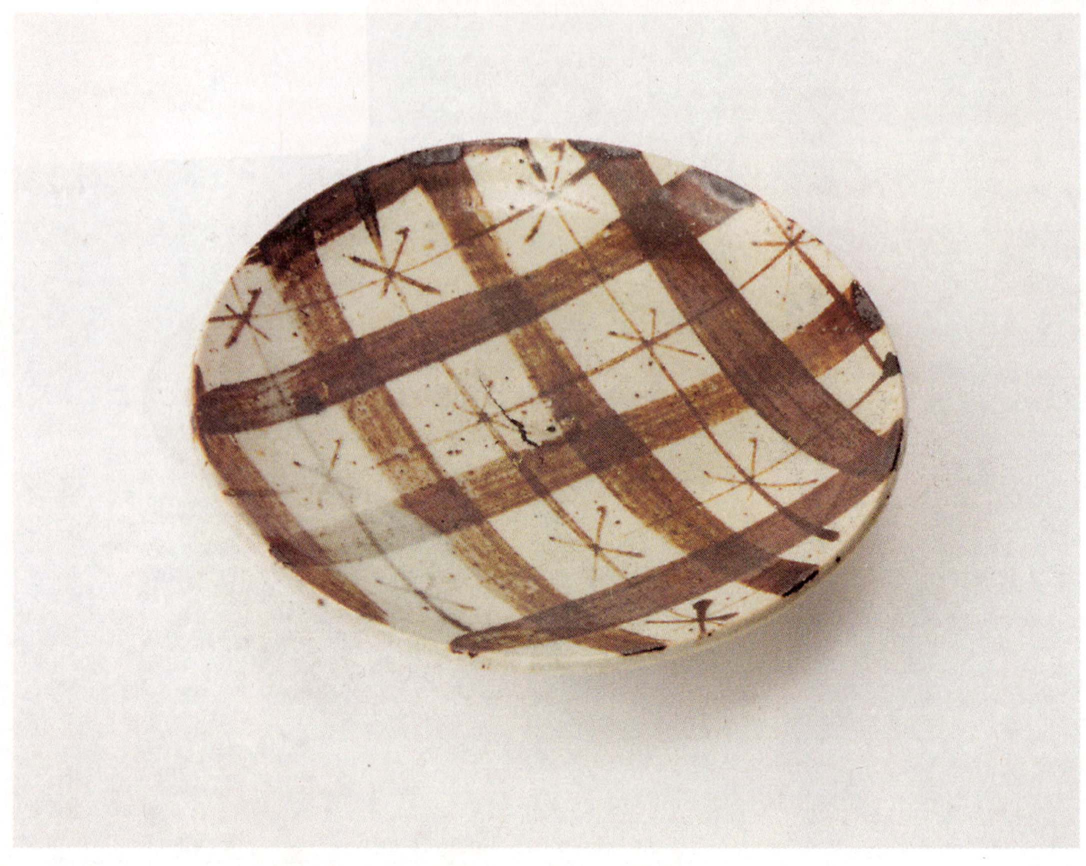

Kitaoji Rosanjin
Untitled, c. 1950
Ceramic plate
2 x 7 inches
4.4 x 17.8 cm

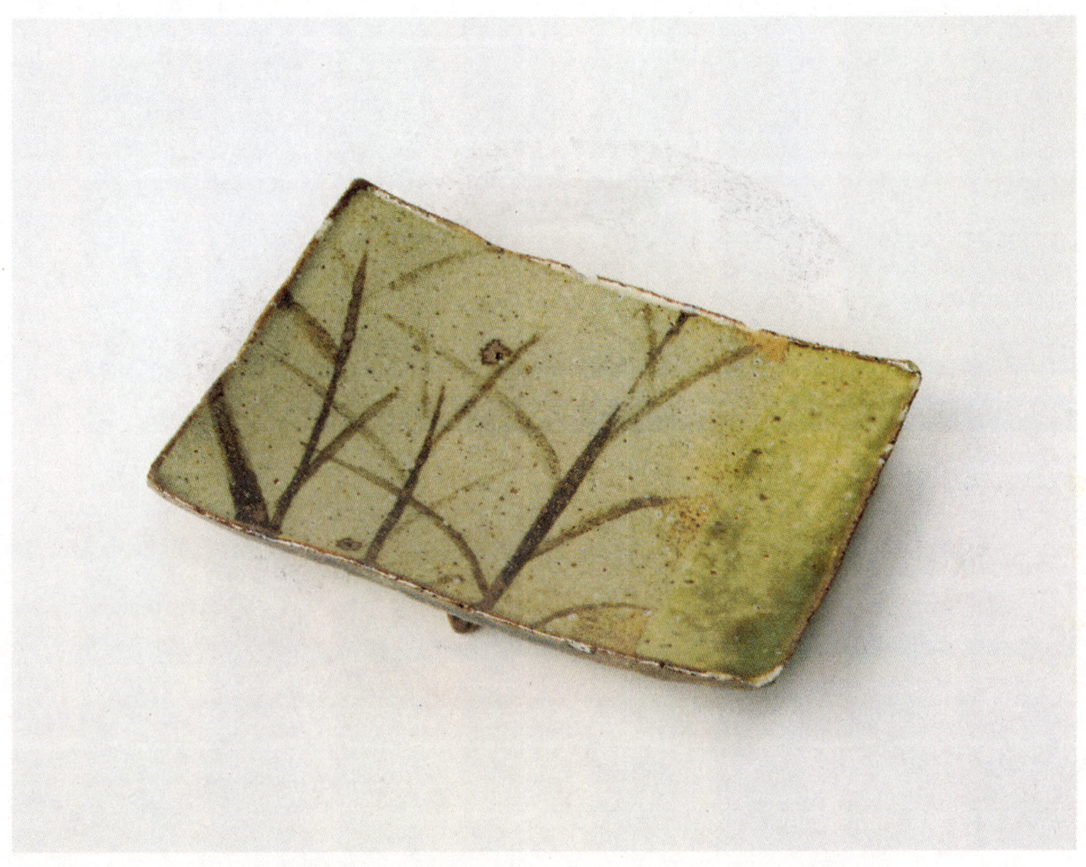

Kitaoji Rosanjin
Untitled, c. 1950
Ceramic plate
1 x 6.5 x 5 inches
2.5 x 16.5 x 12.1 cm

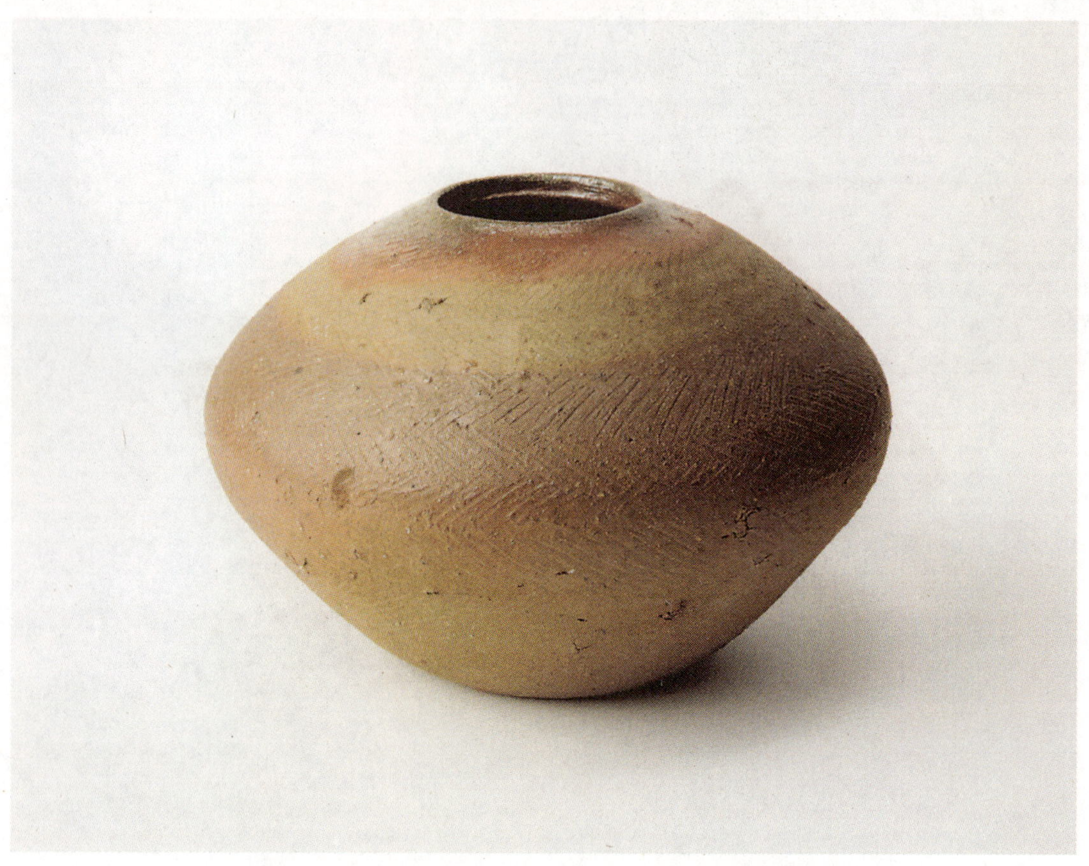

Toyo Kaneshige
Untitled, c. 1950
Ceramic vase
10 x 7 inches
25 x 18 cm

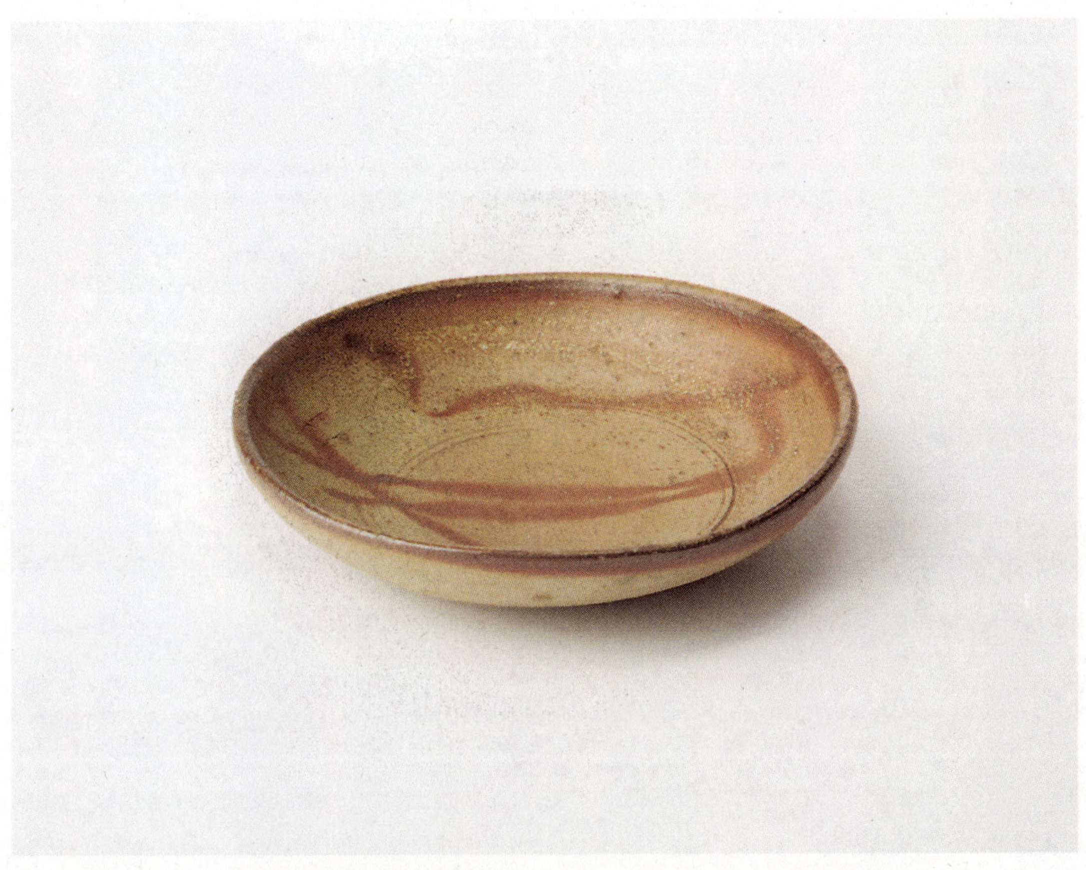

Toyo Kaneshige
Untitled, c. 1950
Ceramic bowl
2 x 9 inches
5.1 x 22.2 cm

Cups,
plates,
bowls
&
sculptures

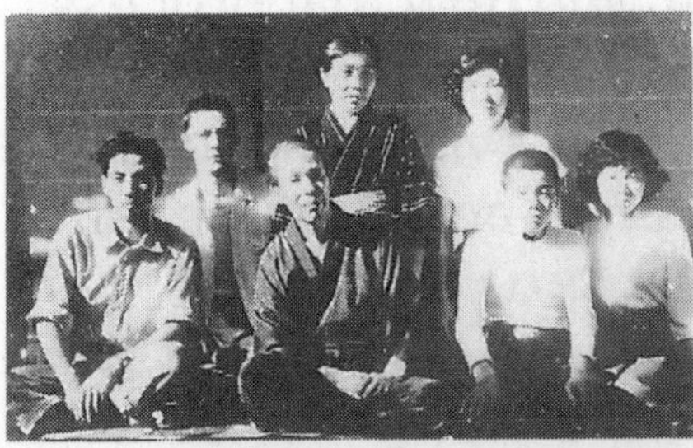

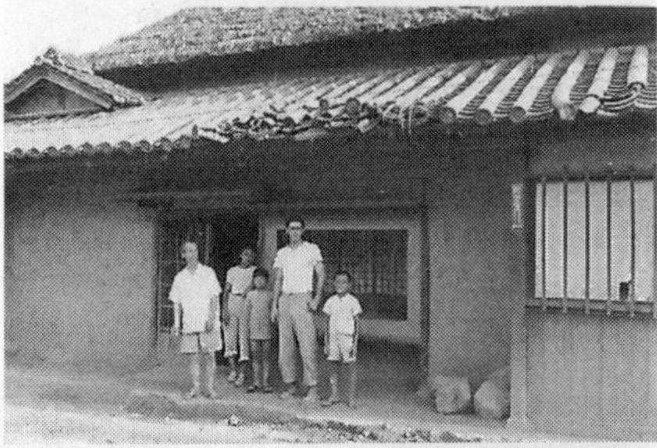

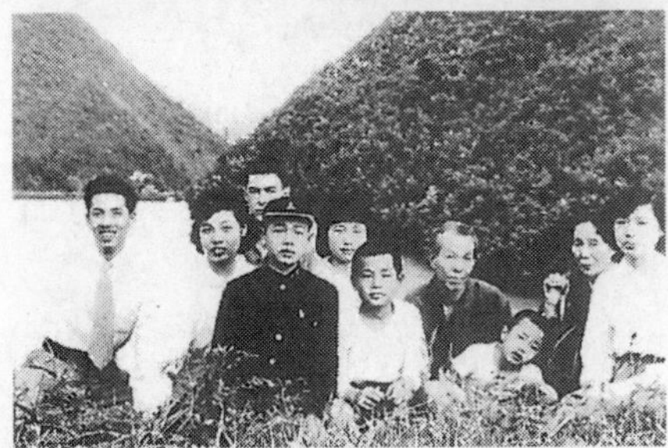

JB Blunk with Toyo Kaneshige
and family in Bizen, Japan, circa 1952

California-based artist JB Blunk created an extensive body of work in carved wood, stone, cast bronze, painting, jewelry and clay. Ignoring the traditional separation of sculpture and furniture, he worked without a conception of fixed categories, and his attitude towards these classifications calls to mind the Japanese disregard for the distinction between art and craft.

Coincidentally, Blunk's career as an artist began in Japan. After graduating from UCLA, where he had studied ceramics with Laura Andreson, he was drafted into the Korean War, which enabled him leave from his post for visits to Japan. Once there, he was hoping to meet the renowned Japanese potter Shoji Hamada, whose work he had seen in an exhibit at Scripps College. In 1952, Blunk was rewarded with a chance encounter at Takumi, a *mingei* (folk craft) shop, with the prominent sculptor Isamu Noguchi. On hearing of his interests, Noguchi introduced him to the famed potter Kitaoji

Rosanjin, who engaged Blunk as an apprentice for several months. From Rosanjin's studio, he went to Bizen for 18 months in order to work in the ceramic studio of another Living National Treasure, Toyo Kaneshige.

The very first exhibition of Blunk's artwork was in Japan in 1954. Curated by Noguchi, the show took place at Chuo Koron Gallery in Tokyo, and the proceeds from the exhibition went towards the purchase of Blunk's return ticket to the United States. In his review of the exhibition, painter and art historian Saburo Hasegawa wrote: 'Pottery is a craft which has been highly developed in Japan and is noted for its elaborate technical achievements. Yet, the Japanese potters have never forgotten the profound charm of the simple and primitive. Blunk has found [the Bizen ware] an inspiring medium for self-expression and has gained the power of directness.'

By the time Blunk returned to California in 1954, he was thoroughly immersed in the Japanese stoneware tradition. His deep commitment to the physical process of making, and how that process might guide the creative outcome, is evident in both his ceramics and large-scale wood sculpture. Working primarily with his hands, Blunk created art that exhibited an acknowledgement and respect for the material — an inclination reinforced by his training in Japan.

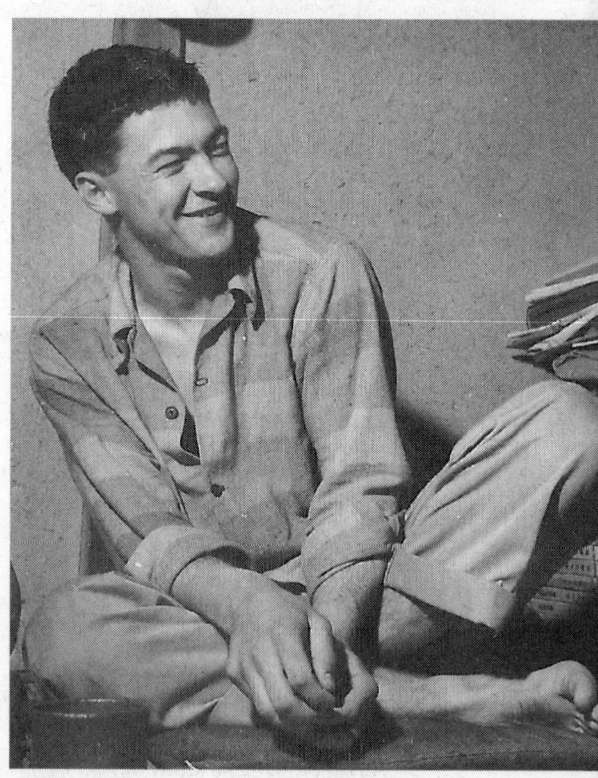

JB Blunk, Bizen, Japan, circa 1952

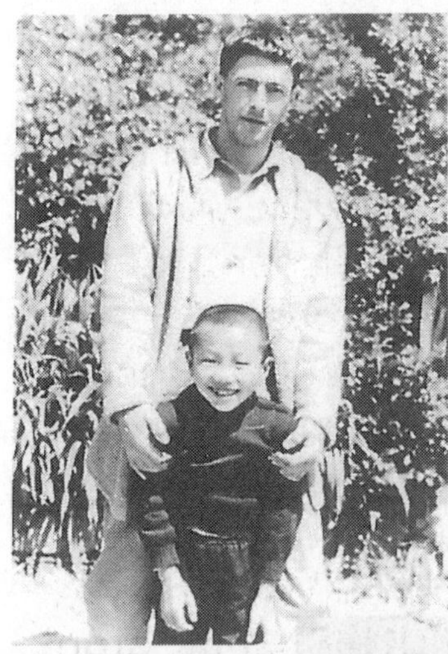

JB Blunk with Toyo Kaneshige's son, Bizen, Japan, circa 1952

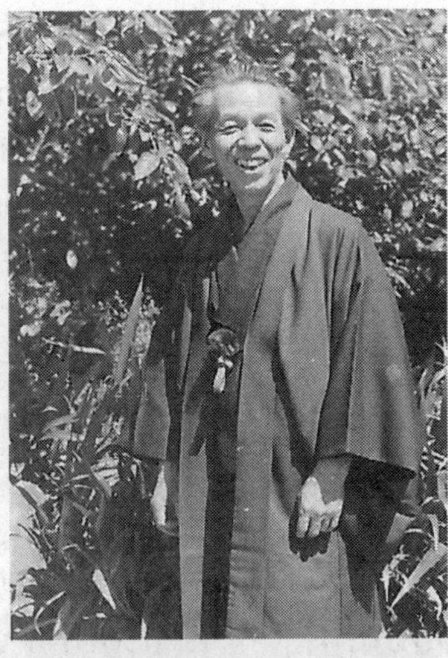

Toyo Kaneshige, Bizen, Japan, circa 1952

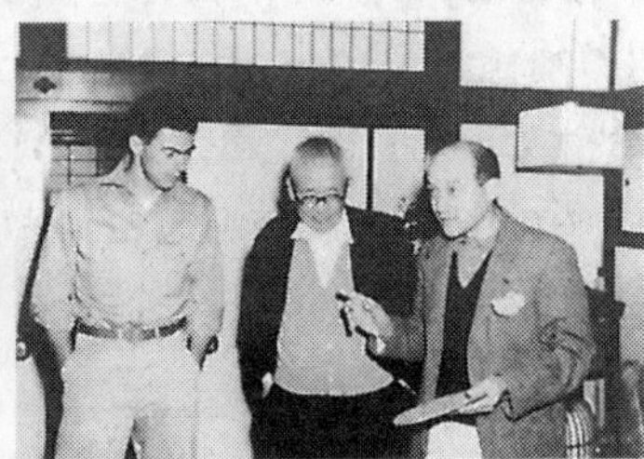

JB Blunk, Kitaoji Rosanjin and Isamu Noguchi at Rosanjin's house, Japan, 1952

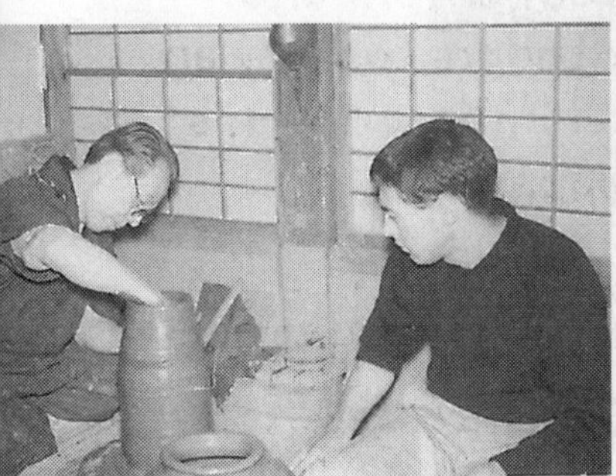

JB Blunk assisting Toyo Kaneshige in the studio, Bizen, Japan, circa 1952

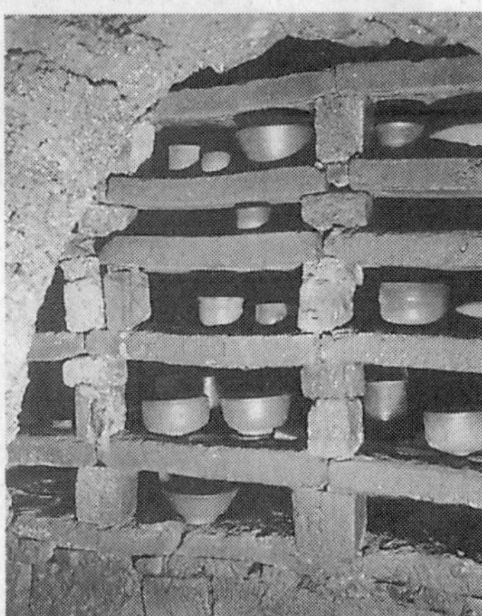

The kiln at Toyo Kaneshige's studio, Bizen, Japan, circa 1952

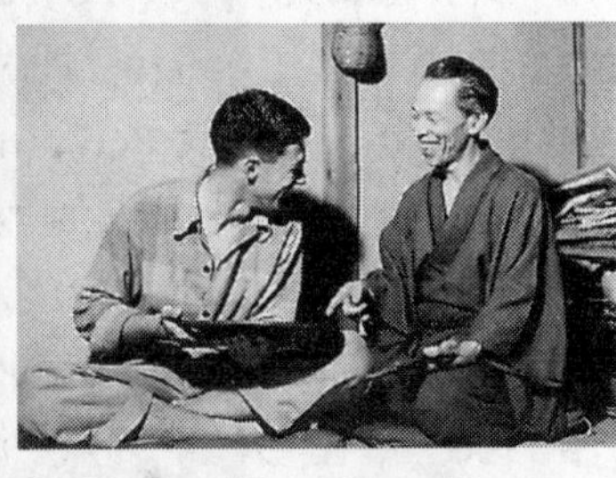

JB Blunk and Toyo Kaneshige in the studio, Bizen, Japan, circa 1952

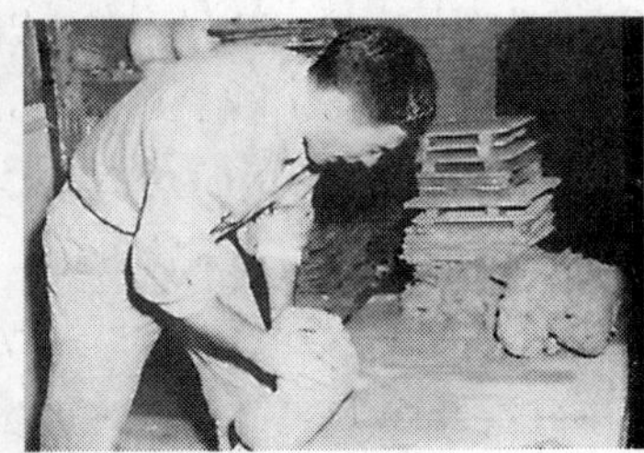

JB Blunk working in Toyo Kaneshige's studio, Bizen, Japan, circa 1952

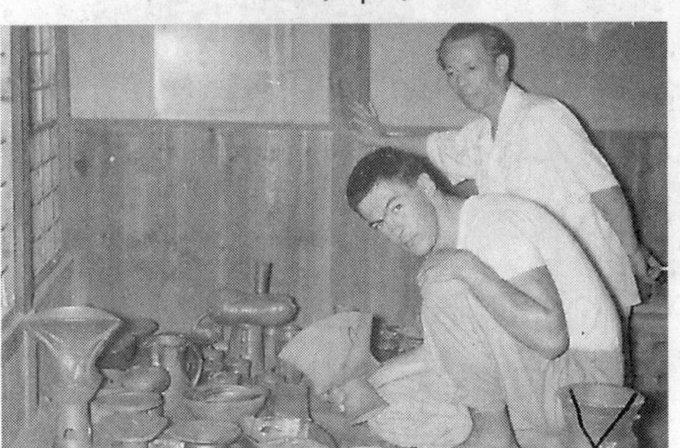

JB Blunk and Toyo Kaneshige in the studio with ceramics made by Blunk, Bizen, Japan, circa 1952

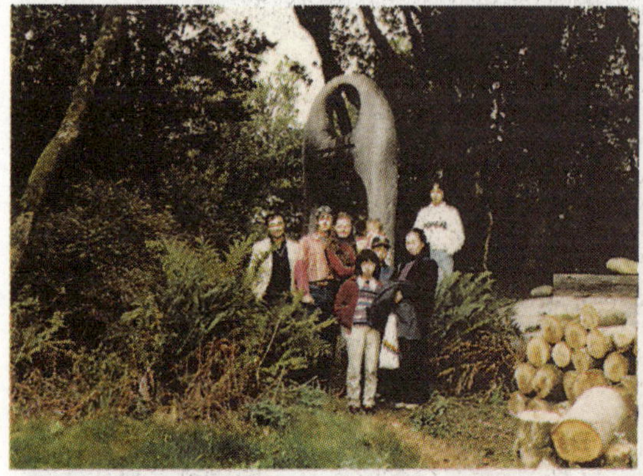

Toyo Kaneshige's family visits the Blunk
family, Inverness, California, 1983

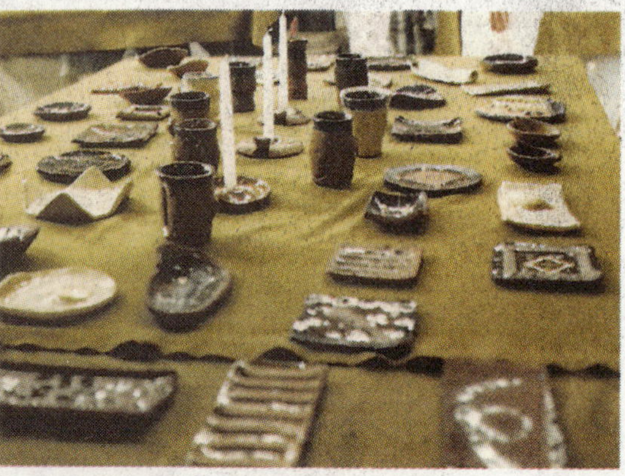

Ceramics made by JB Blunk,
Inverness, California, 1985

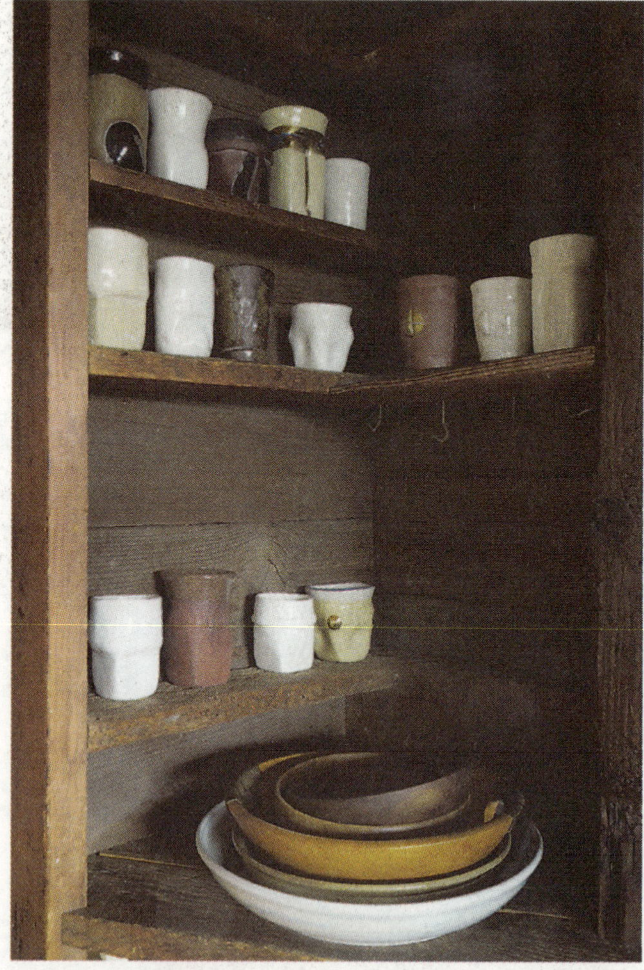

Ceramic cups and wooden bowls at the Blunk
House, Inverness, California, 2014

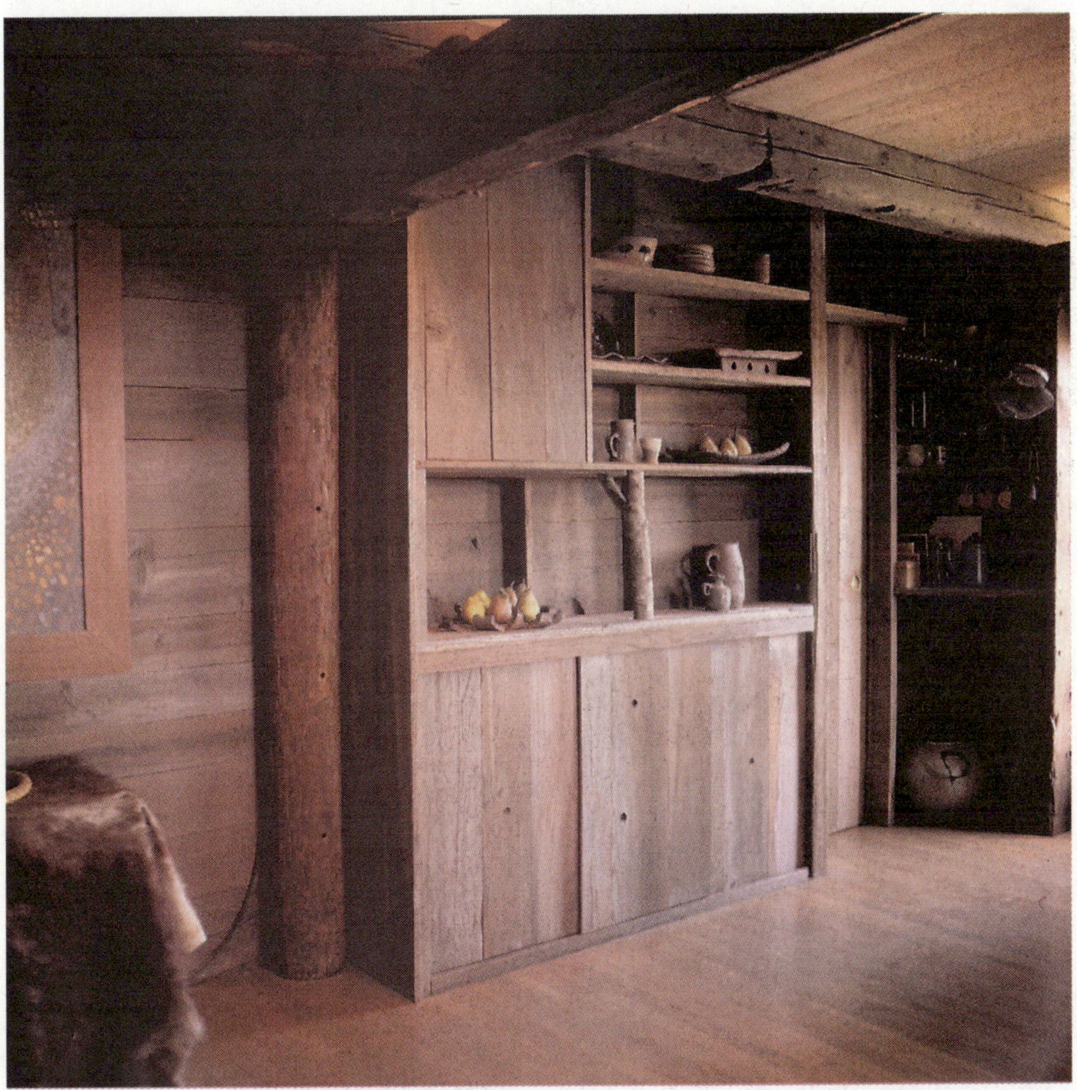

The *tokonoma* in JB Blunk's house,
Inverness, California, 1962

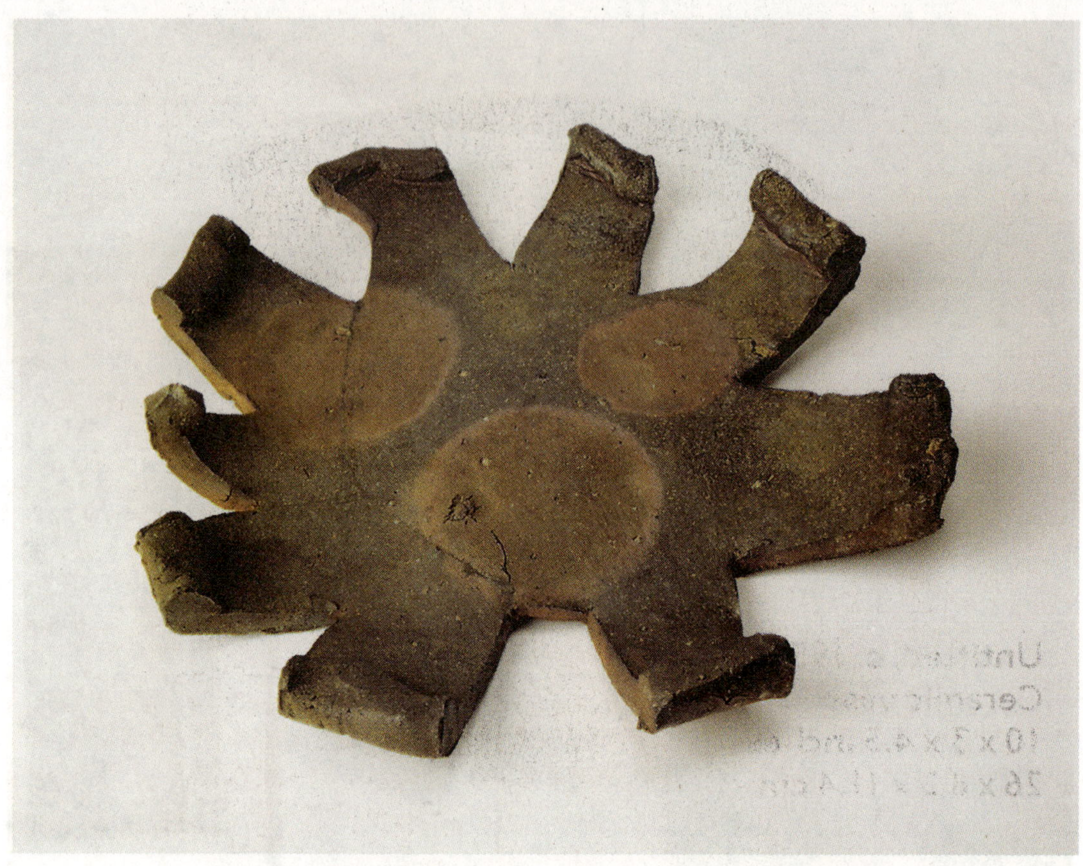

Untitled, c. 1950
Ceramic tray
14 inches
35.6 cm

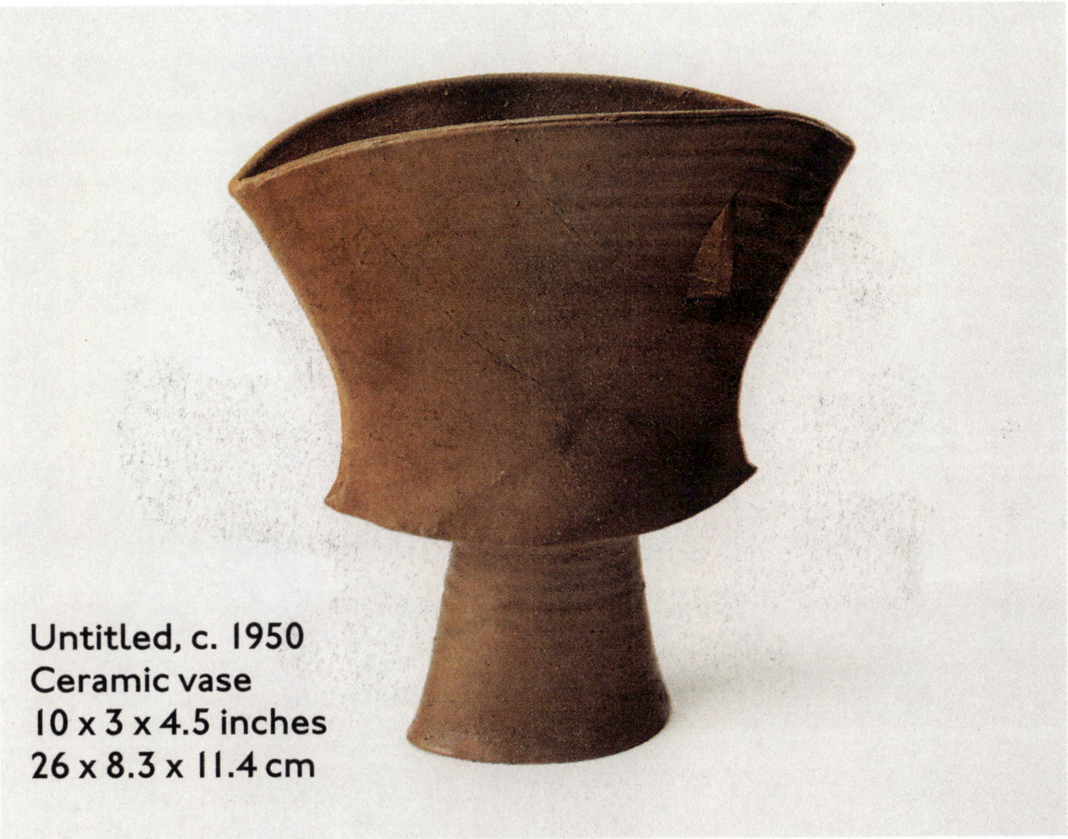

Untitled, c. 1950
Ceramic vase
10 x 3 x 4.5 inches
26 x 8.3 x 11.4 cm

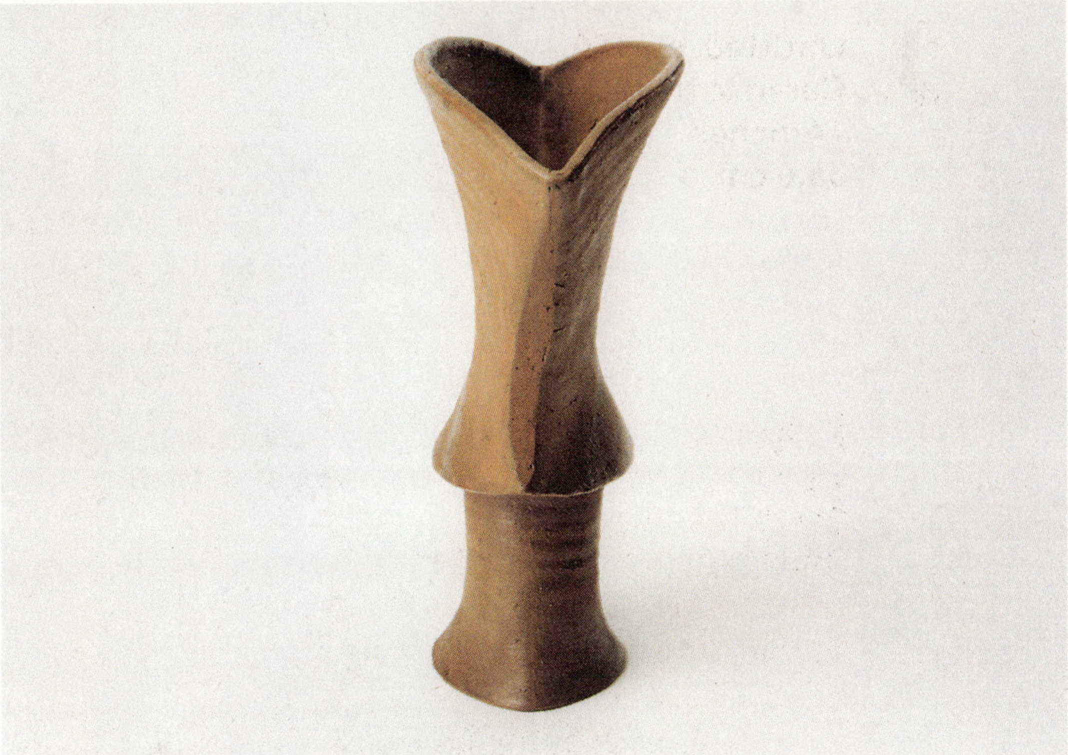

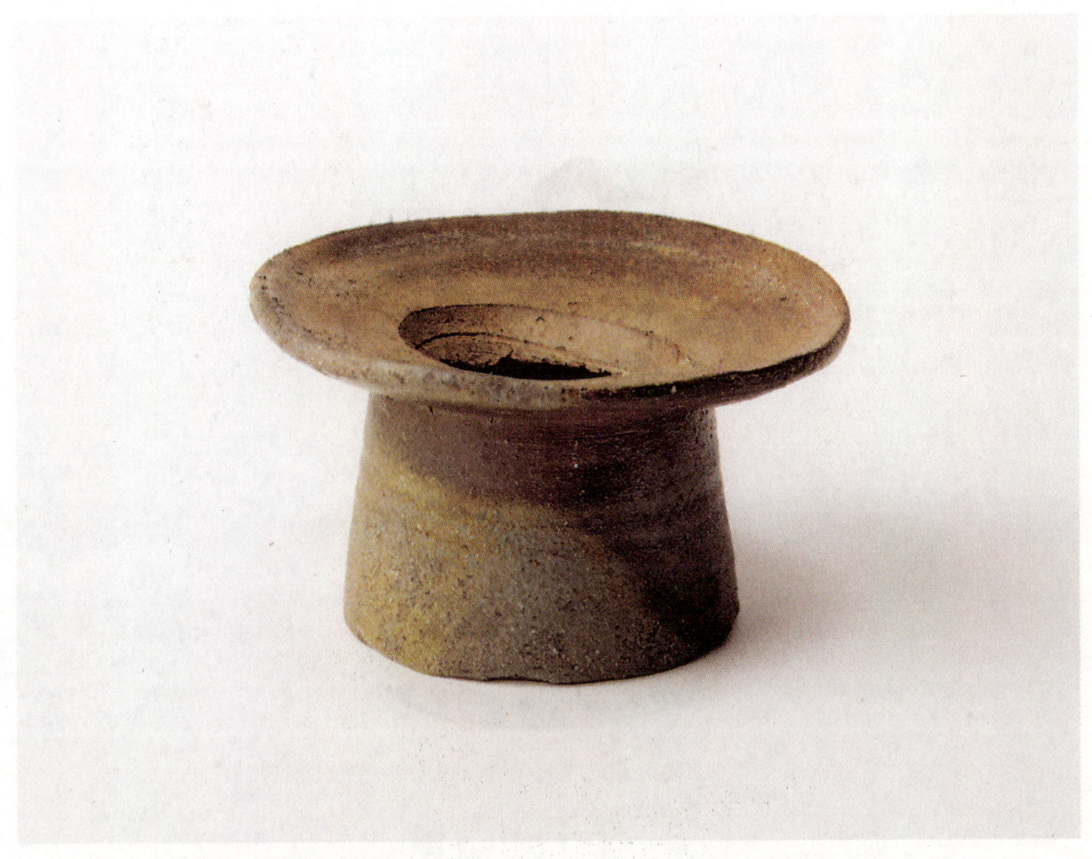

Untitled, c. 1950
Ceramic vase
4 x 6.5 inches
10.2 x 16.5 cm

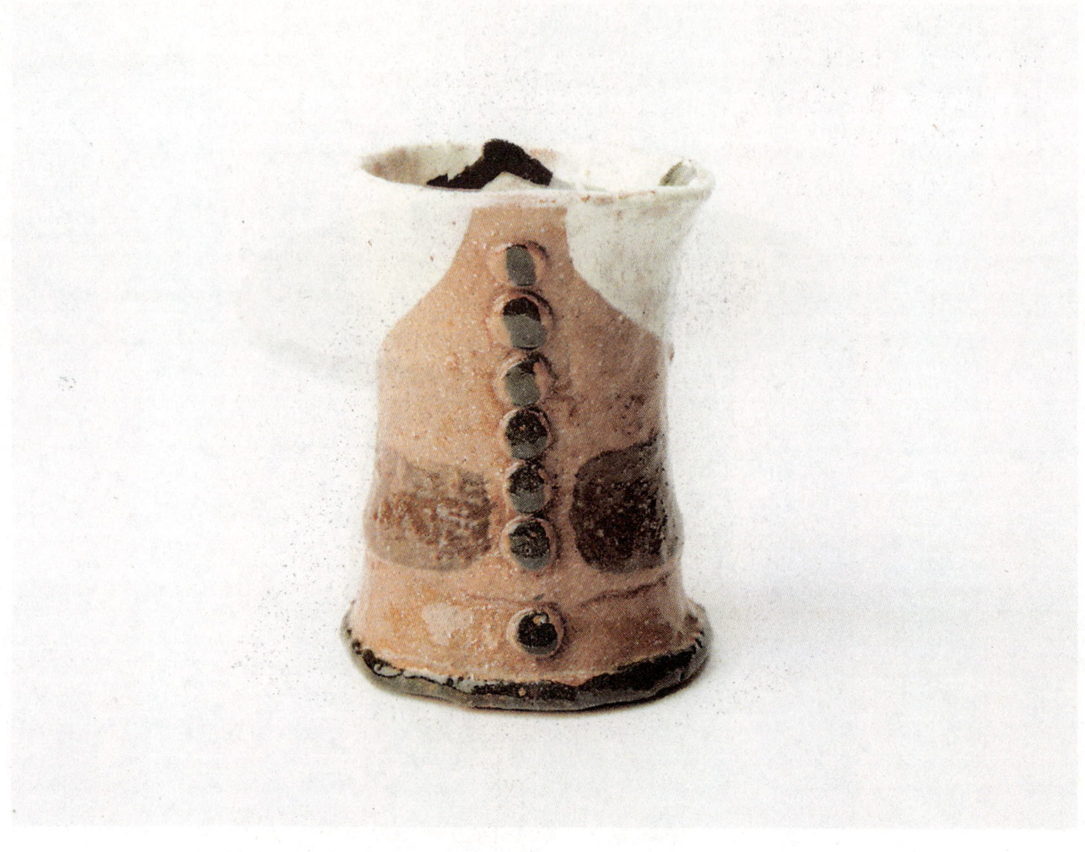

Untitled, c. 1965
Ceramic cup
4.5 x 3 inches
1.4 x 8.3 cm

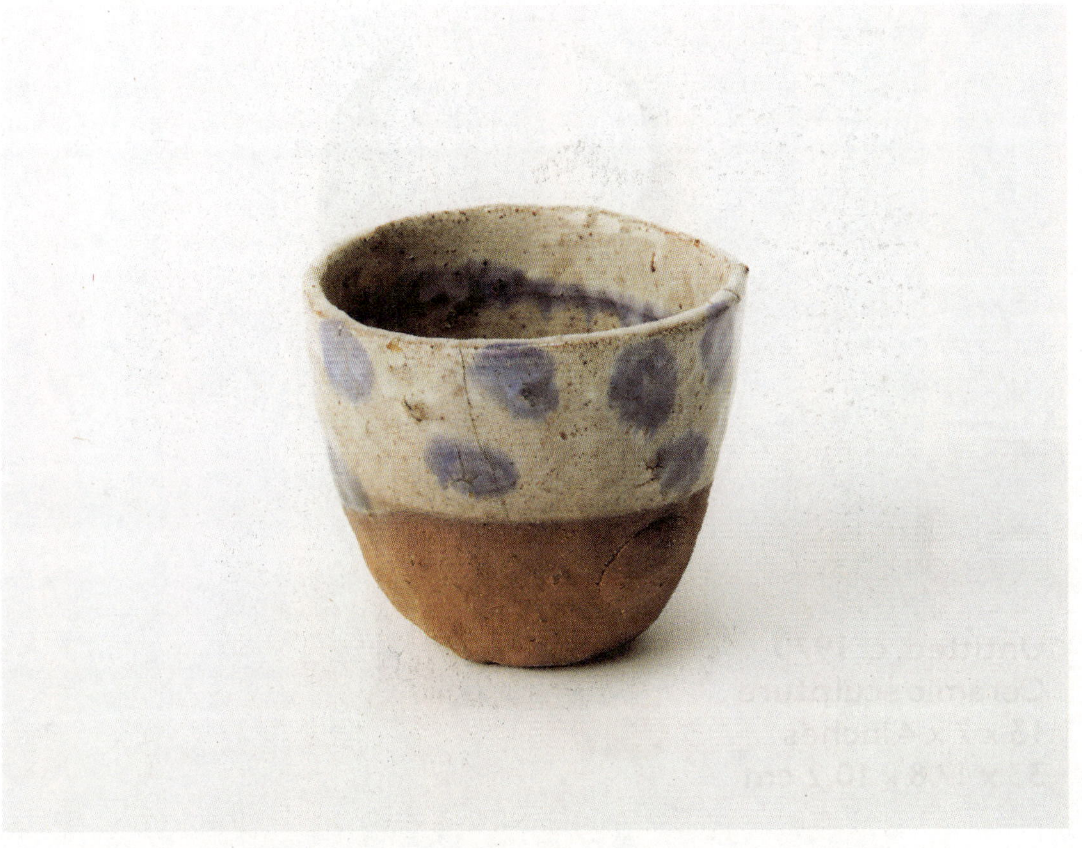

Untitled, c. 1970
Ceramic cup
3 x 3.5 inches
7.6 x 8.9 cm

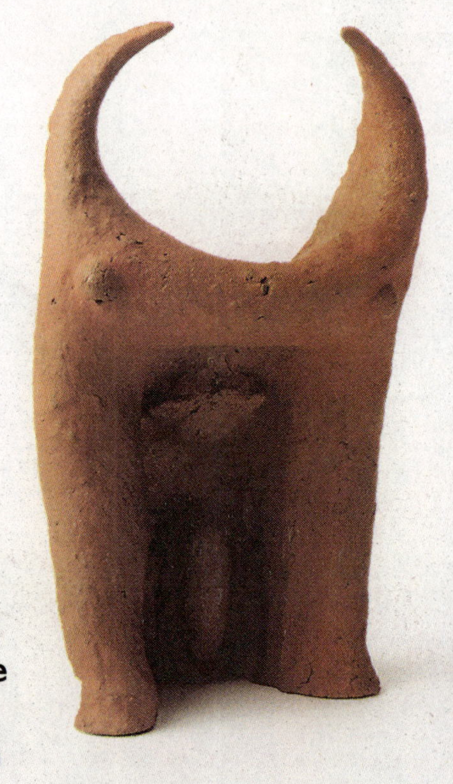

Untitled, c. 1970
Ceramic sculpture
13 x 7 x 4 inches
33 x 17.8 x 10.2 cm

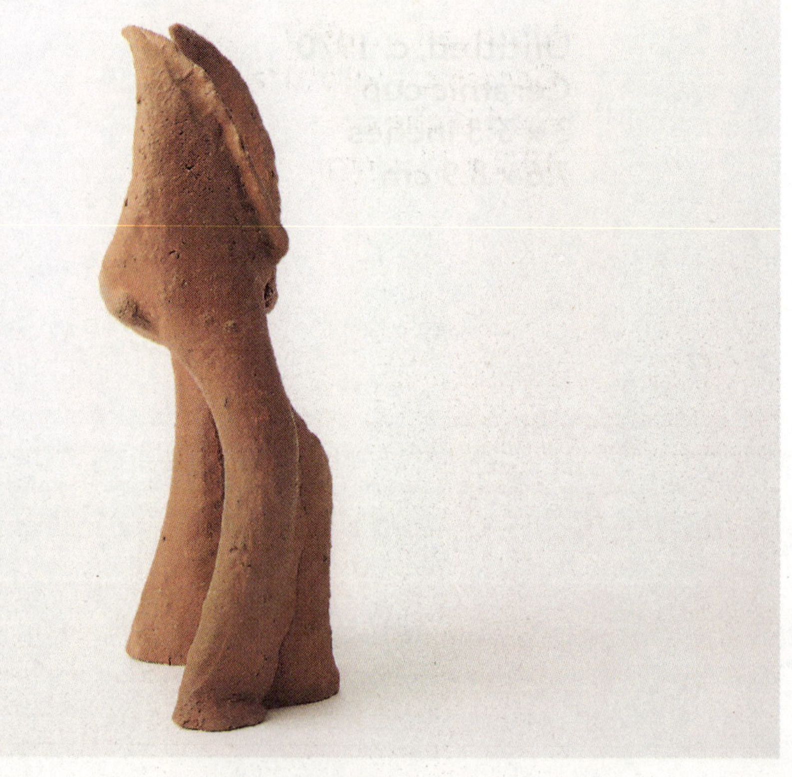

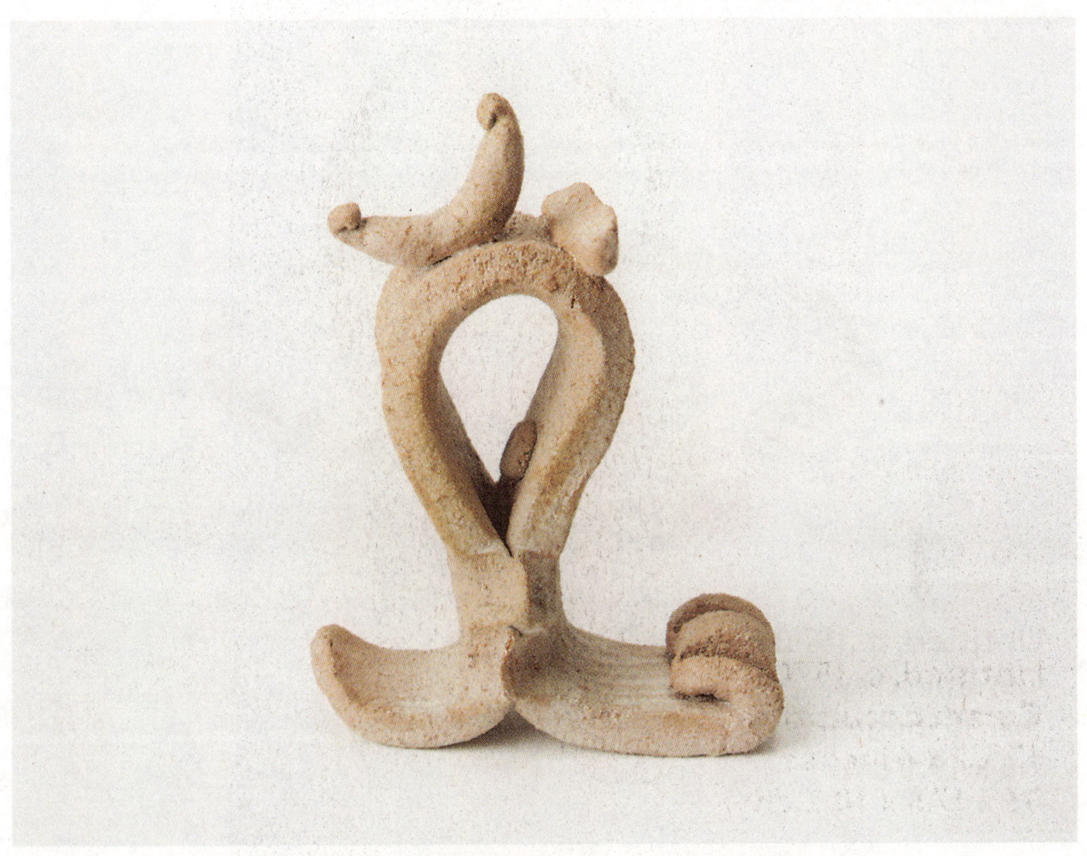

Untitled, c. 1970
Ceramic sculpture
4 x 5 inches
10.2 x 12.7 cm

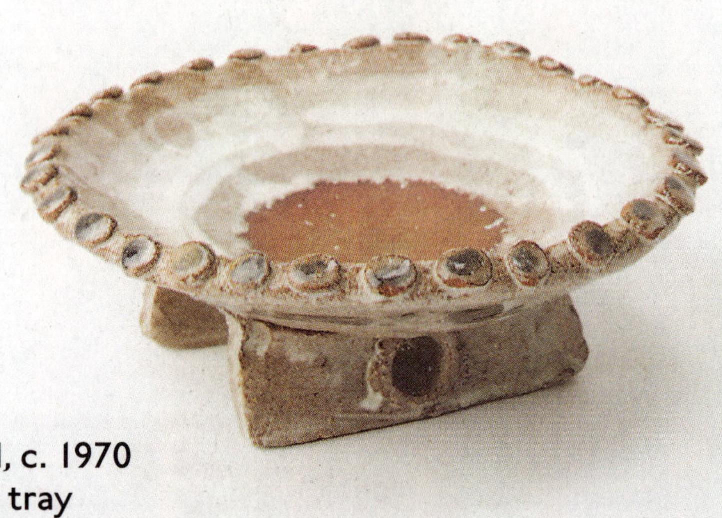

Untitled, c. 1970
Ceramic tray
3 x 7.5 inches
7.6 x 19.1 cm

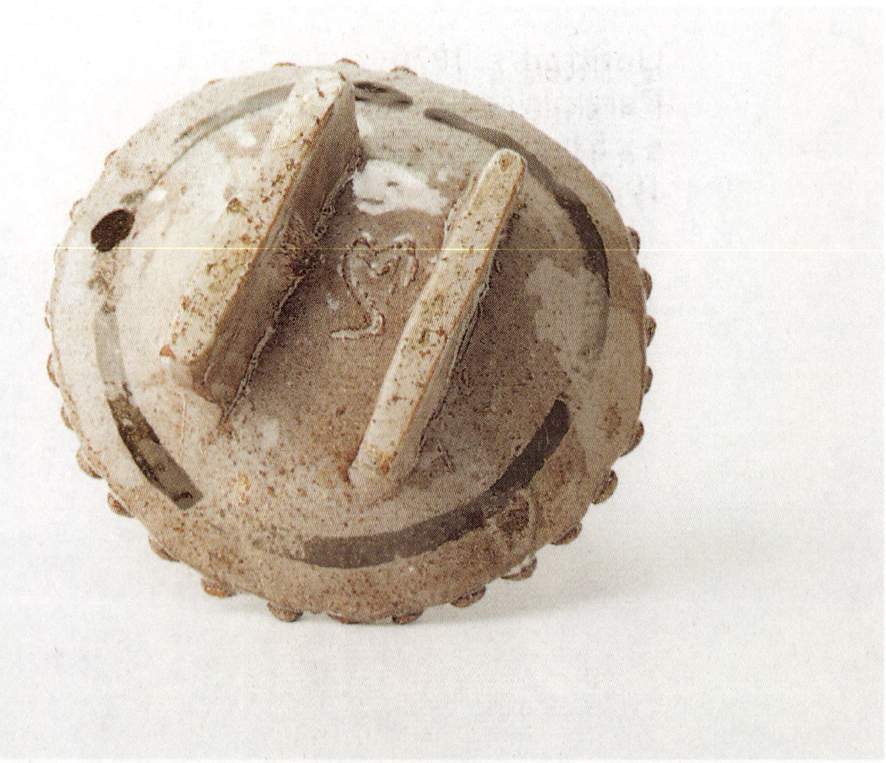

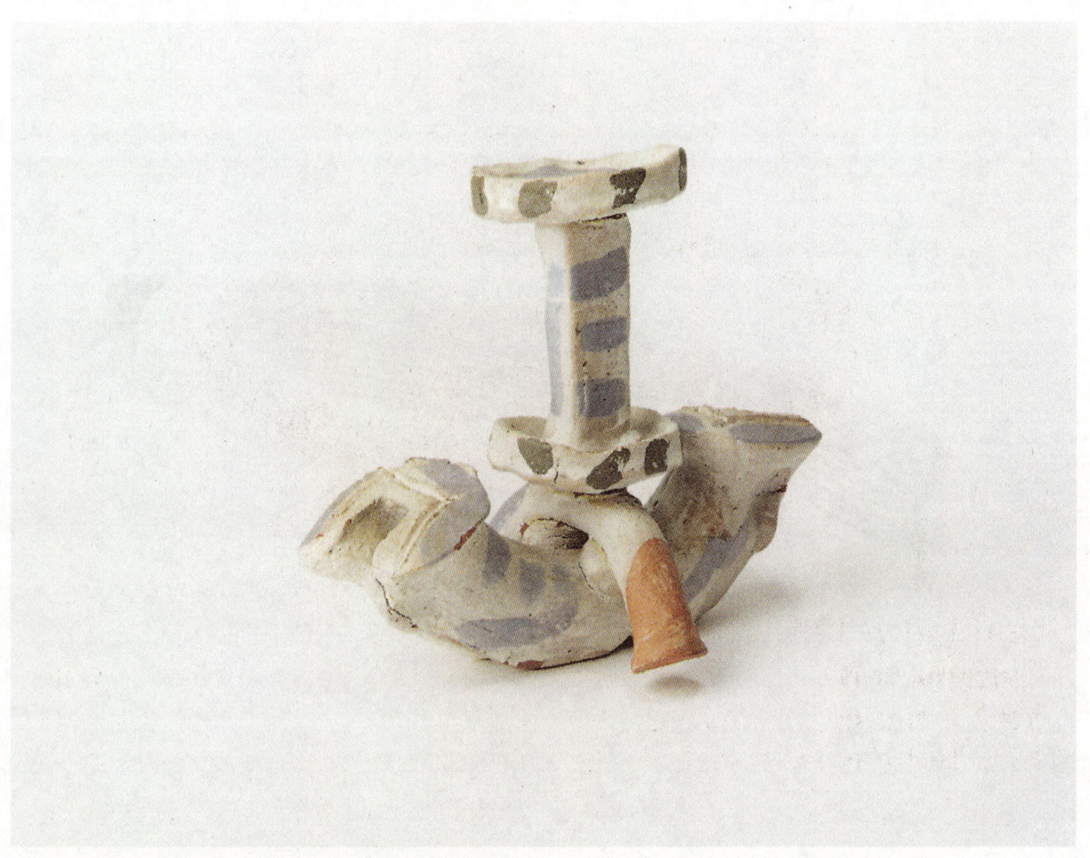

Untitled, c. 1970
Ceramic candleholder
5 x 4 inches
12.7 x 11.4 cm

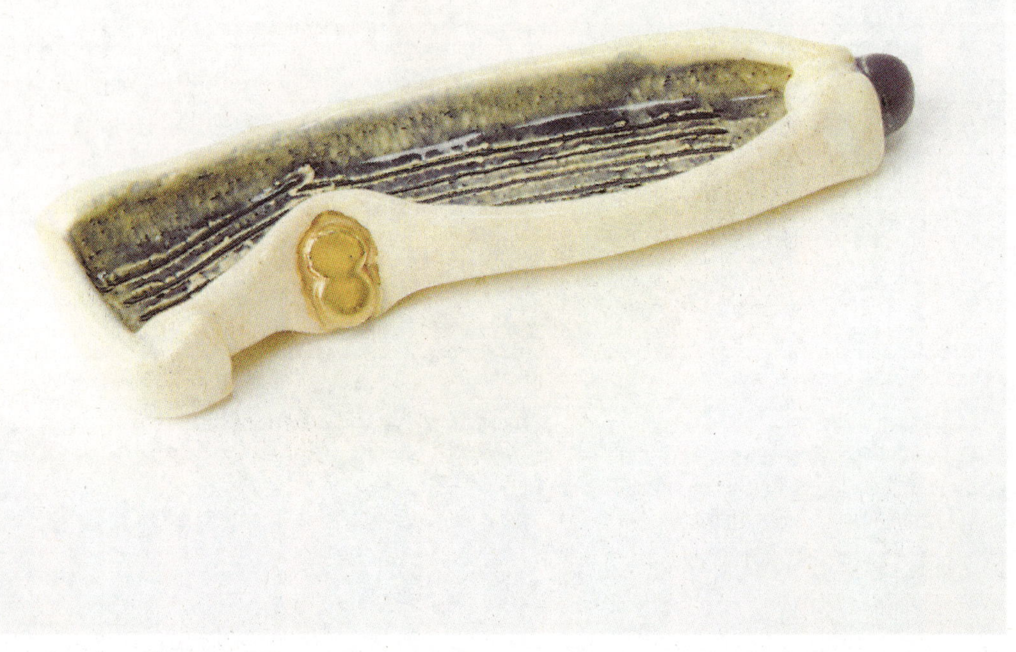

Untitled, c. 1975
Ceramic dish
1 x 7.5 x 6 inches
2.5 x 19.1 x 5.1 cm

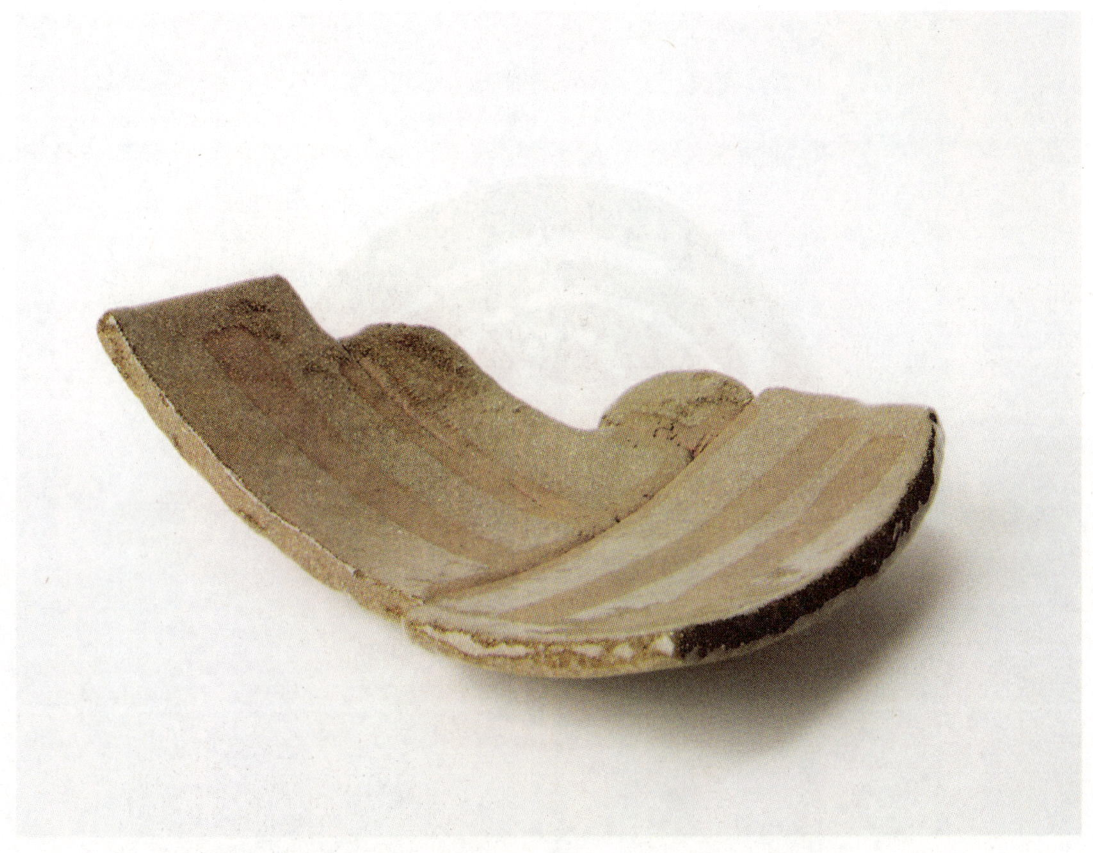

Untitled, c. 1975
Ceramic tray
11 x 8 inches
27.9 x 21 cm

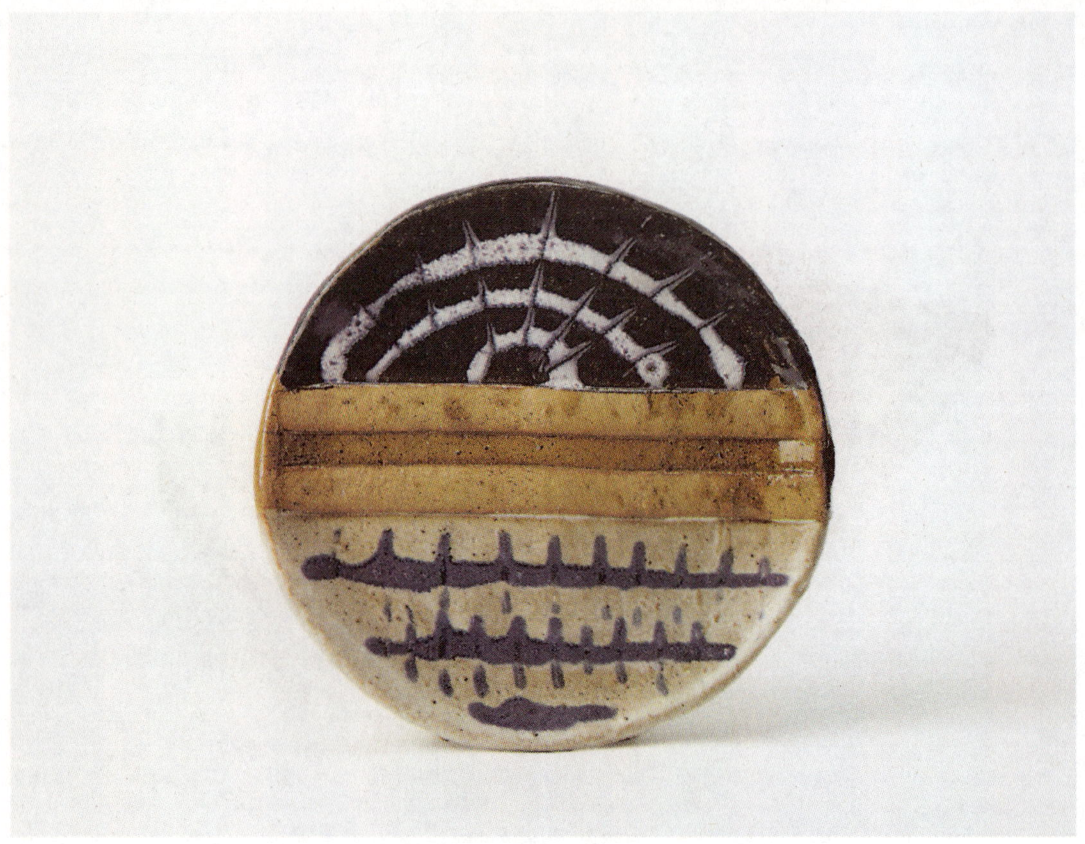

Untitled, c. 1975
Ceramic plate
8 inches
20.3 cm

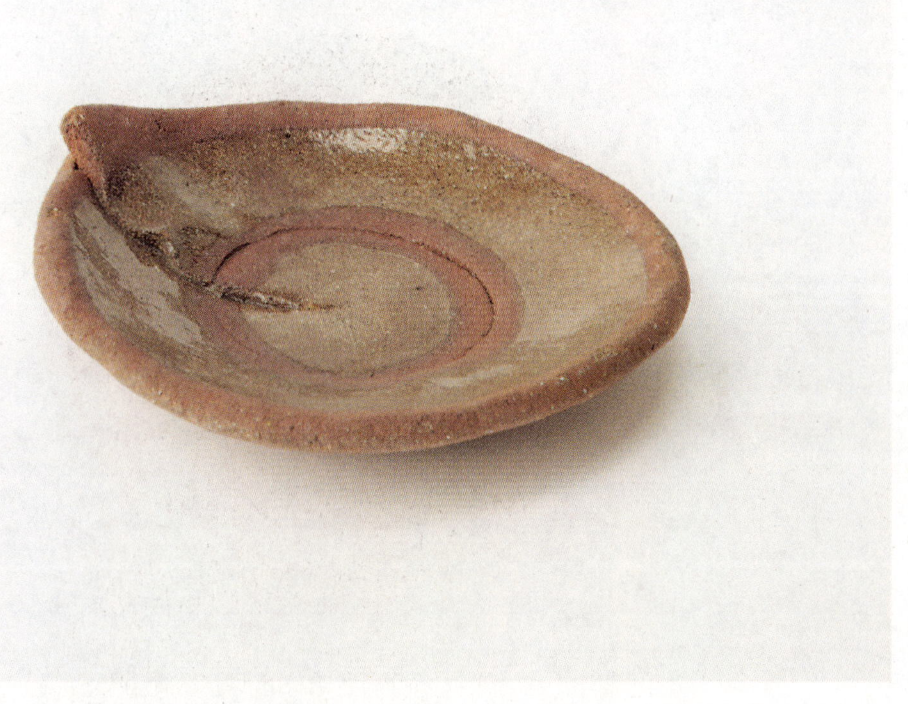

Untitled, c. 1975
Ceramic dish
3.5 x 0.5 inches
9 x 1 cm

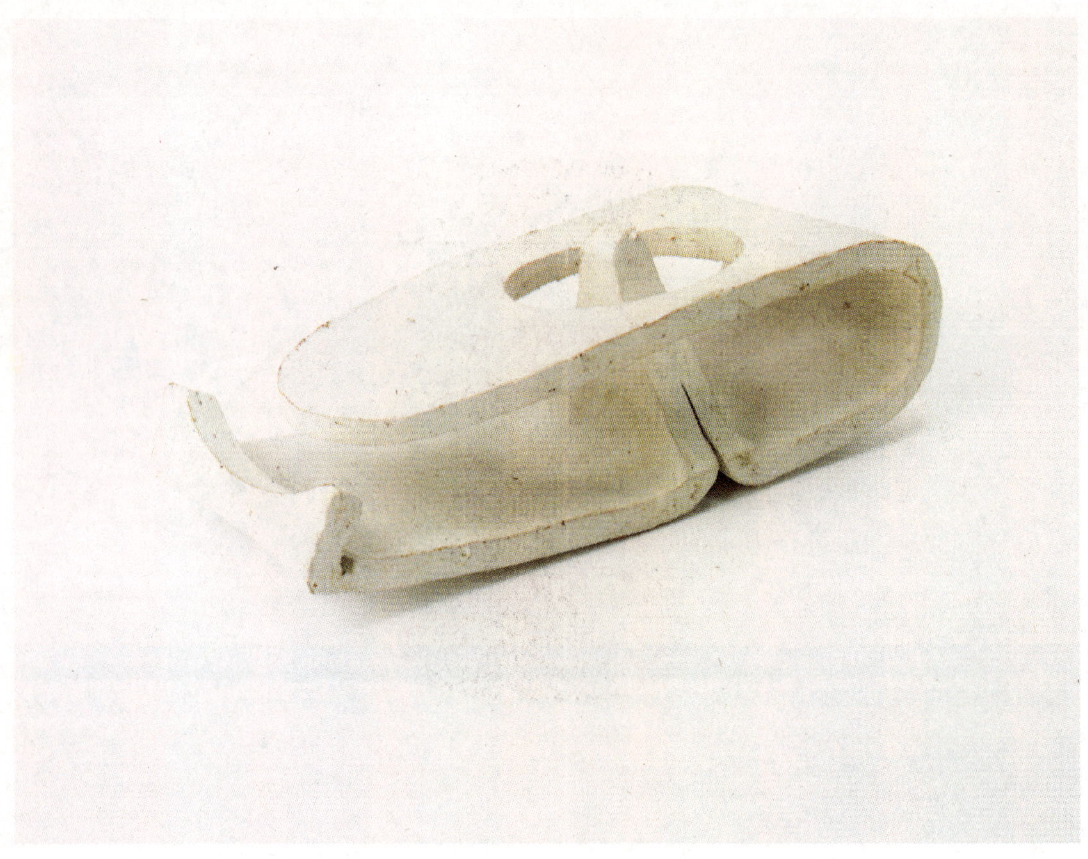

Untitled, c. 1975
Ceramic sculpture
9 x 4 inches
22.9 x 9.5 cm

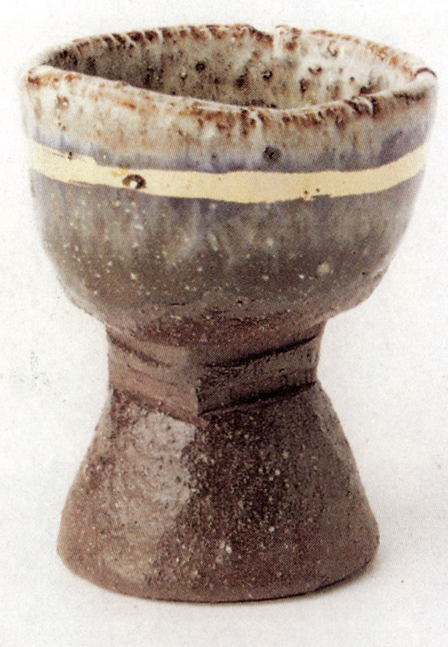

Untitled, c. 1975
Ceramic cup
4 x 3 inches
10.2 x 8.3 cm

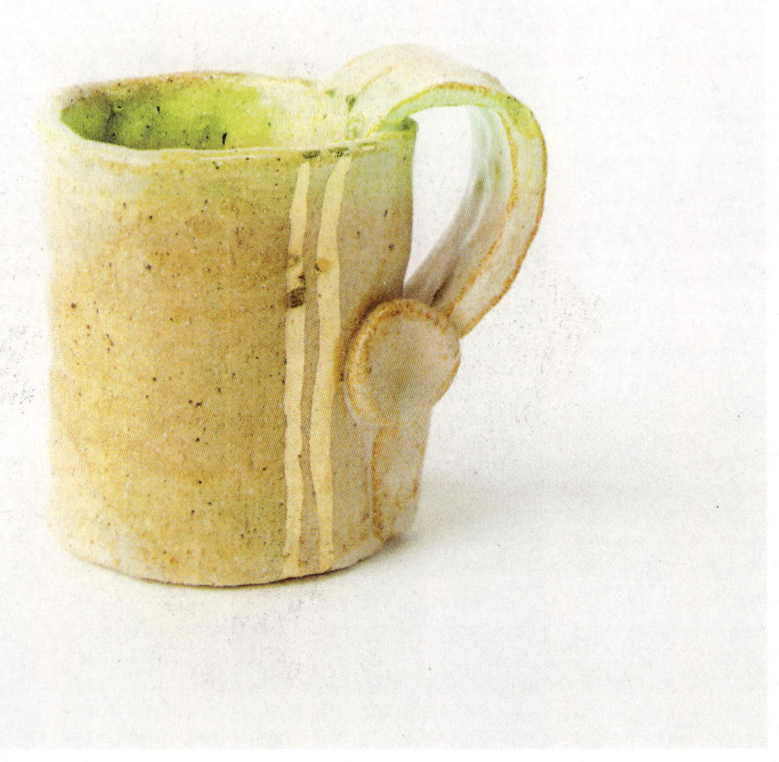

Untitled, c. 1975
Ceramic cup
3.5 x 3.5 x 2.5 inches
8.9 x 8.9 x 6.4 cm

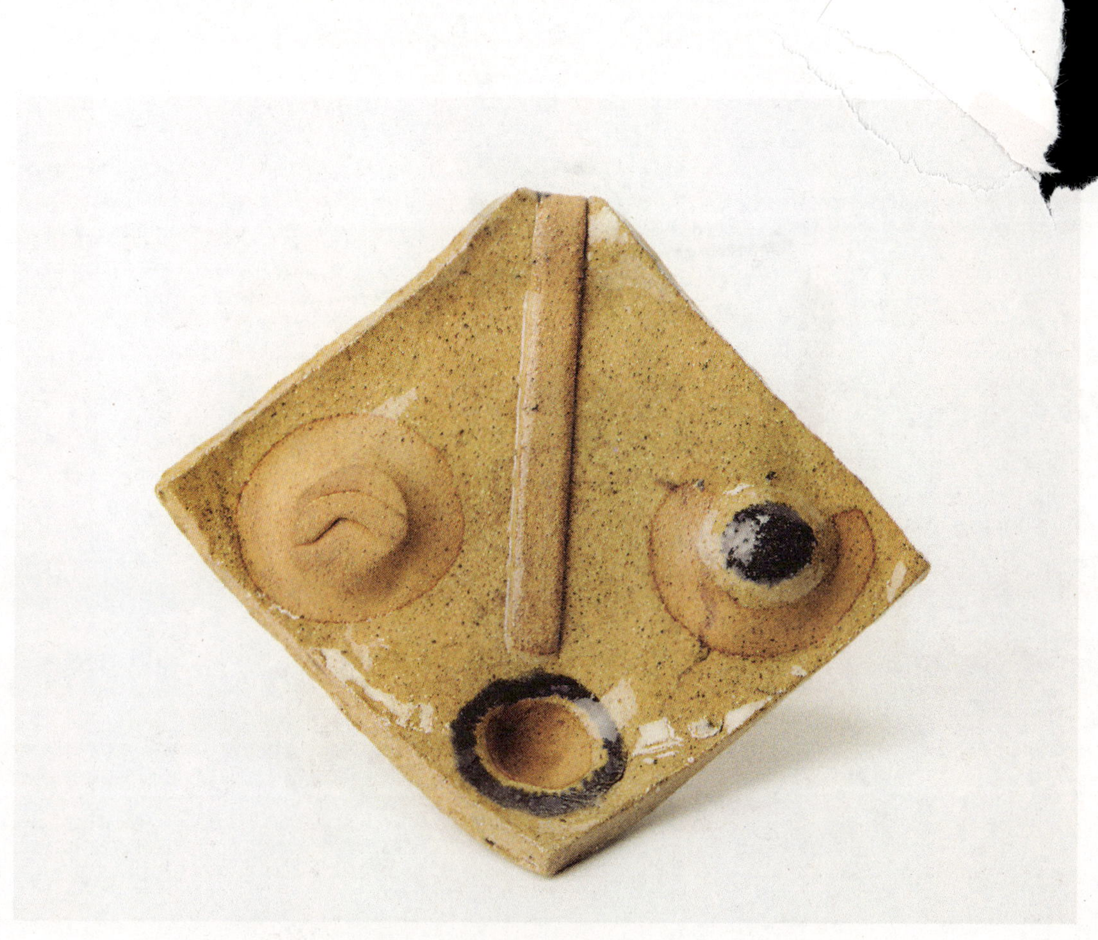

Untitled, c. 1975
Ceramic plate
9 x 10 inches
22.9 x 25.4 cm

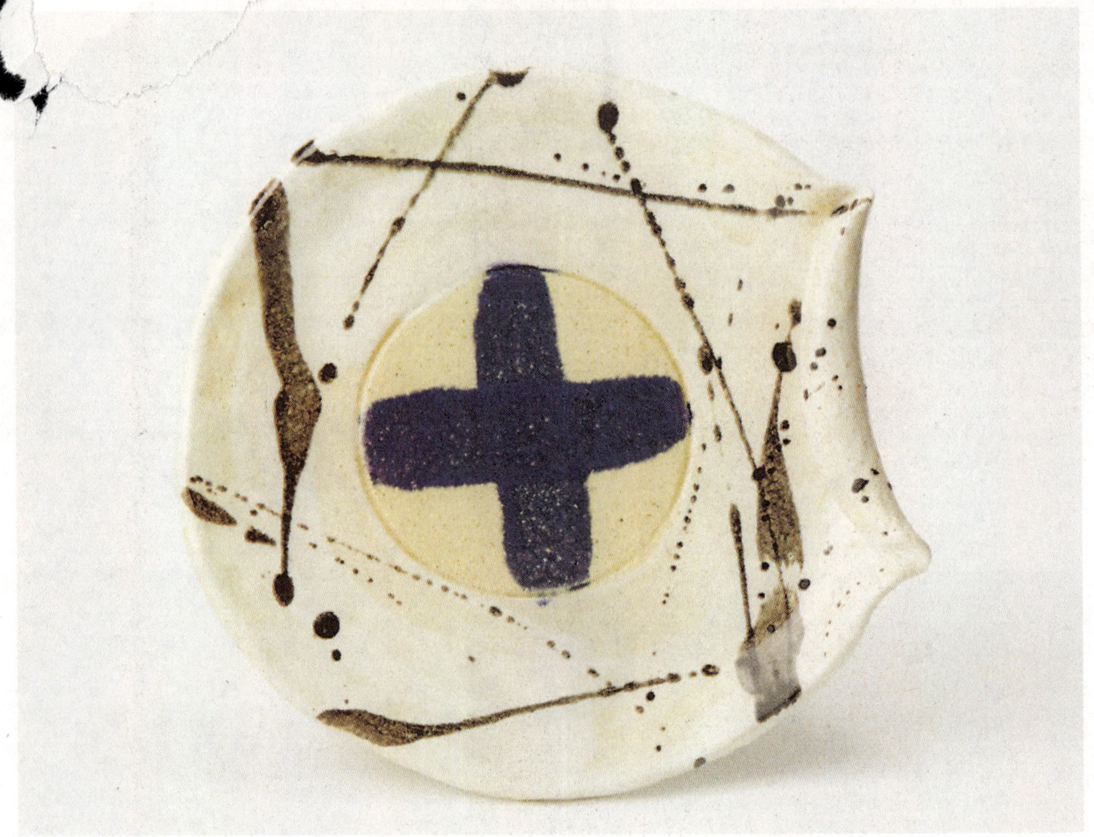

Untitled, c. 1975
Ceramic plate
8.5 inches
21.6 cm

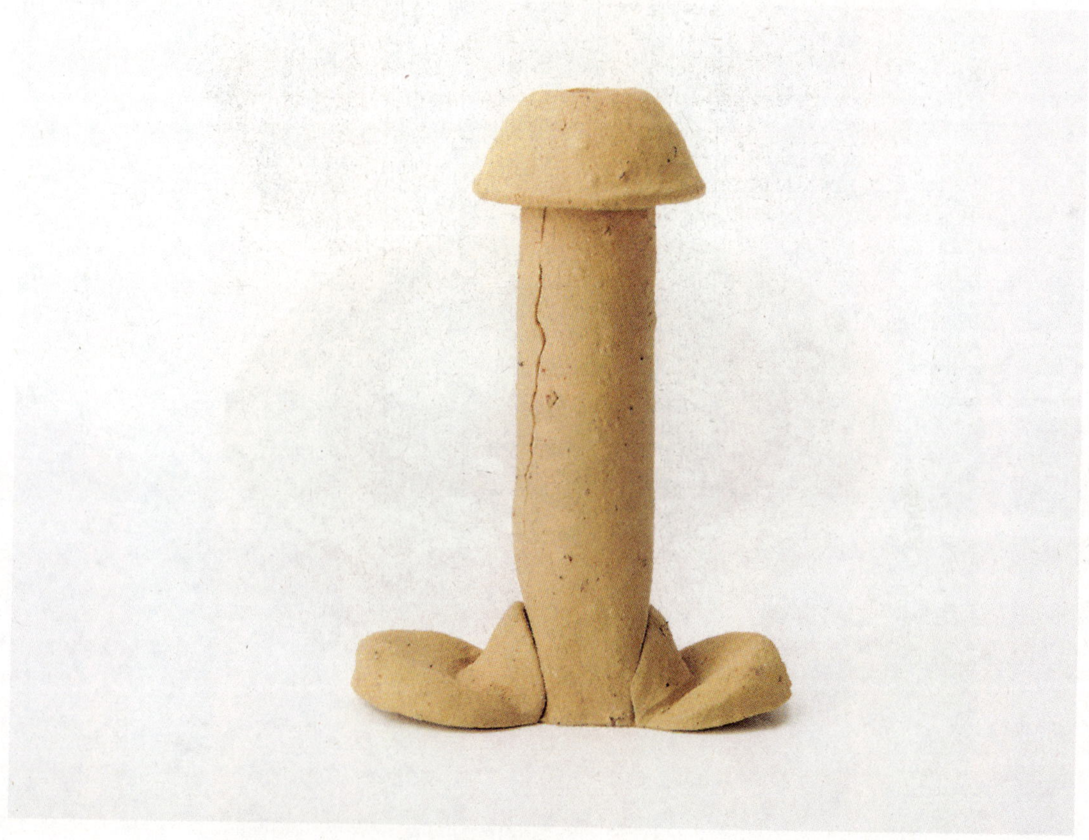

Untitled, c. 1980
Ceramic candleholder
8 x 5.5 inches
20.3 x 14 cm

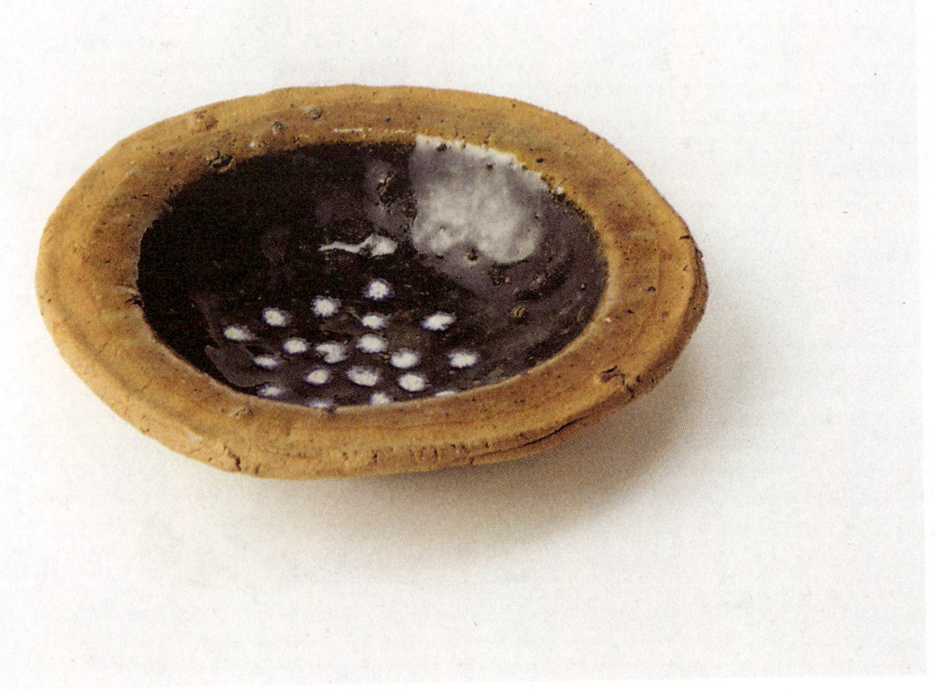

Untitled, c. 1980
Ceramic bowl
1.5 x 6.5 inches
3.8 x 16.5 cm

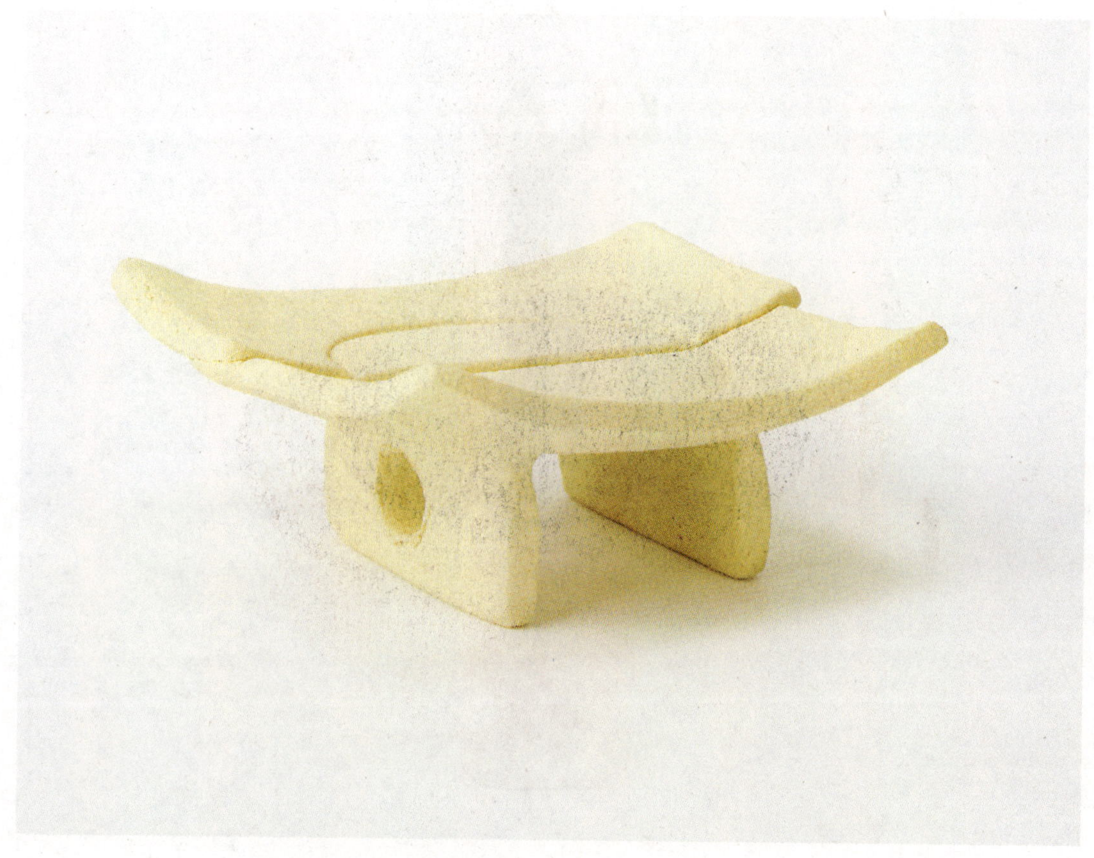

Untitled, c. 1980
Ceramic tray
3 x 8 inches
7 x 20.3 cm

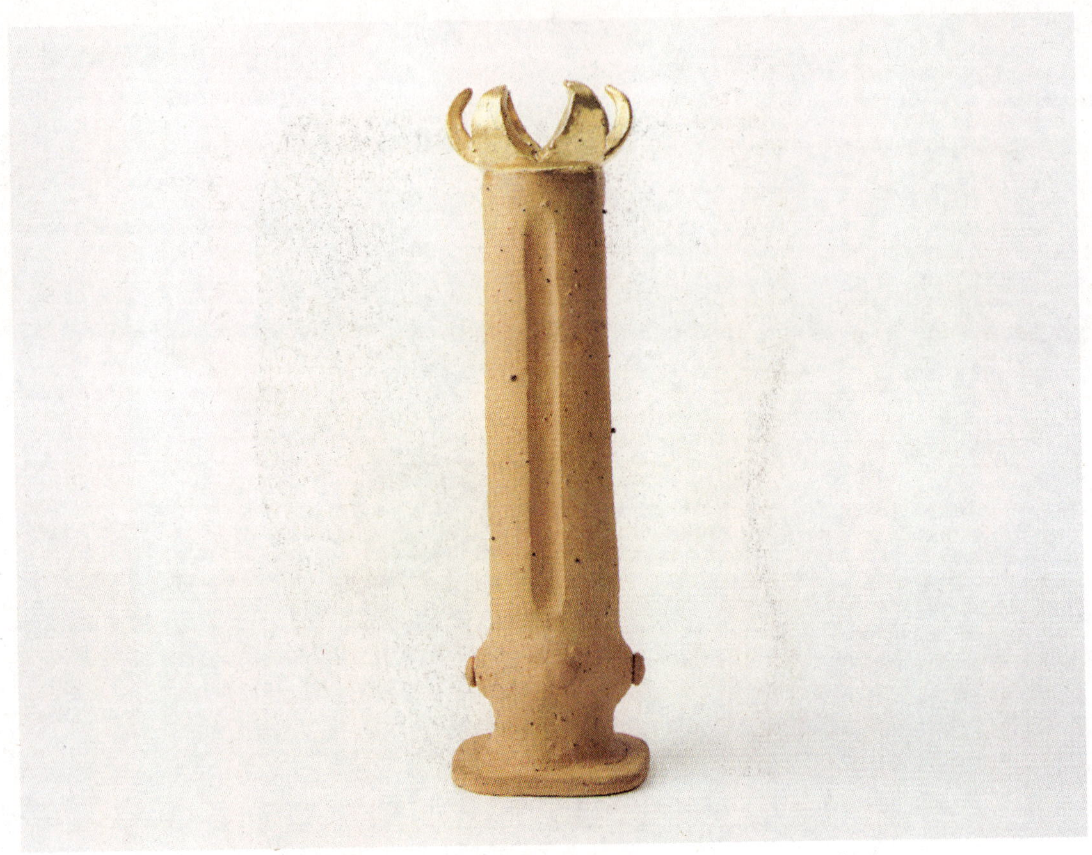

Untitled, c. 1980
Ceramic candleholder
12 x 4 inches
30.5 x 9.5 cm

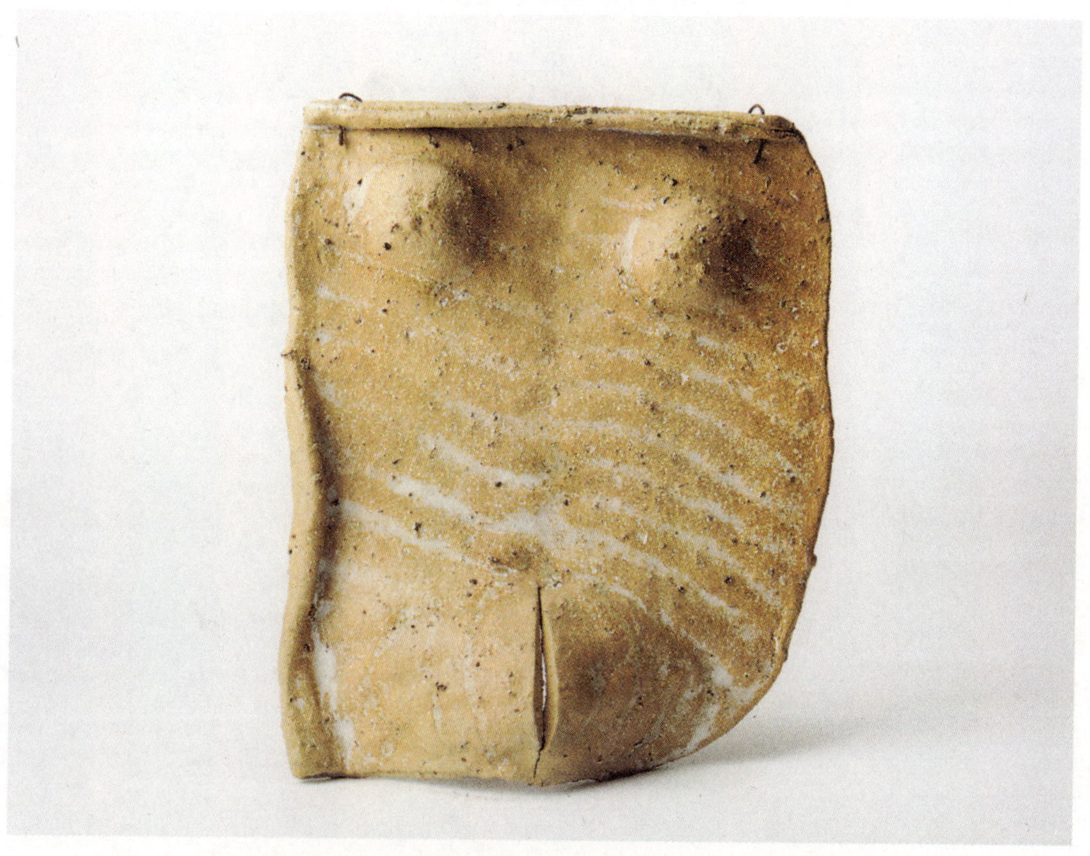

Untitled, c. 1974
Ceramic sculpture
13 x 10.5 inches
33 x 26.7 cm

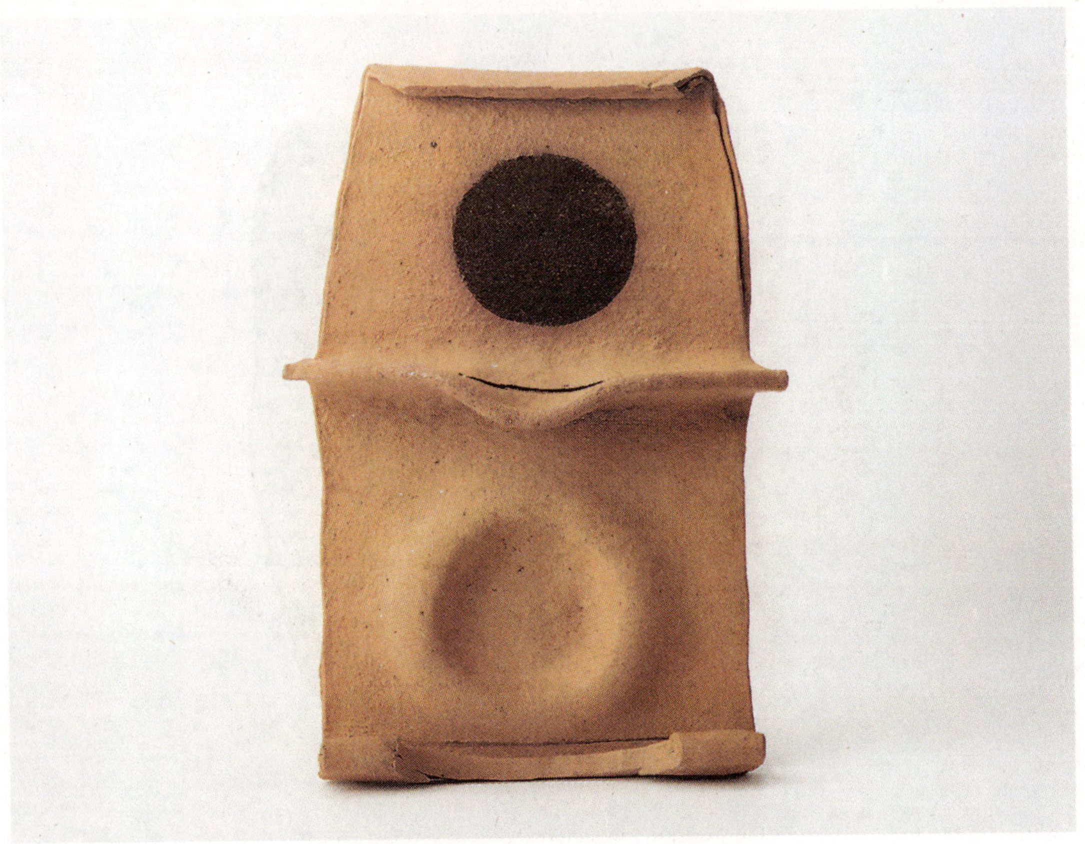

Untitled, c. 1980
Ceramic sculpture
14 x 8.5 inches
35.6 x 21.6 cm

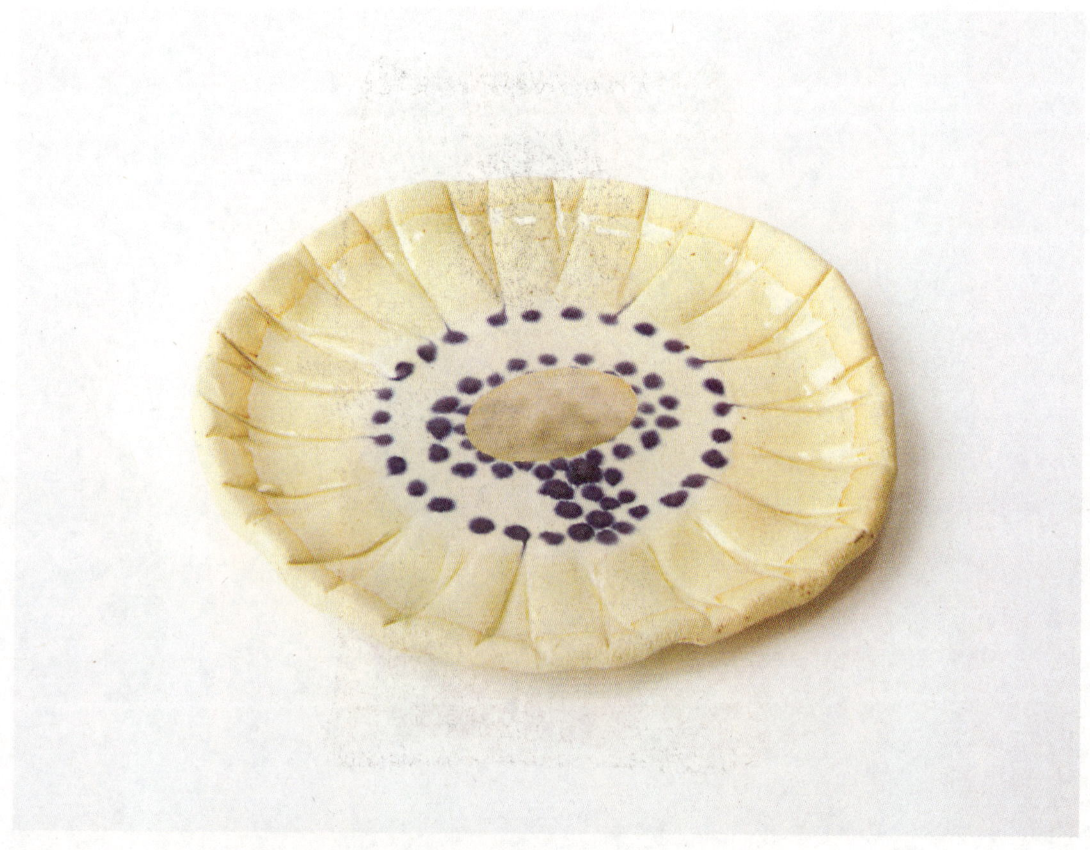

Untitled, c. 1980
Ceramic plate
8 inches
19.7 cm

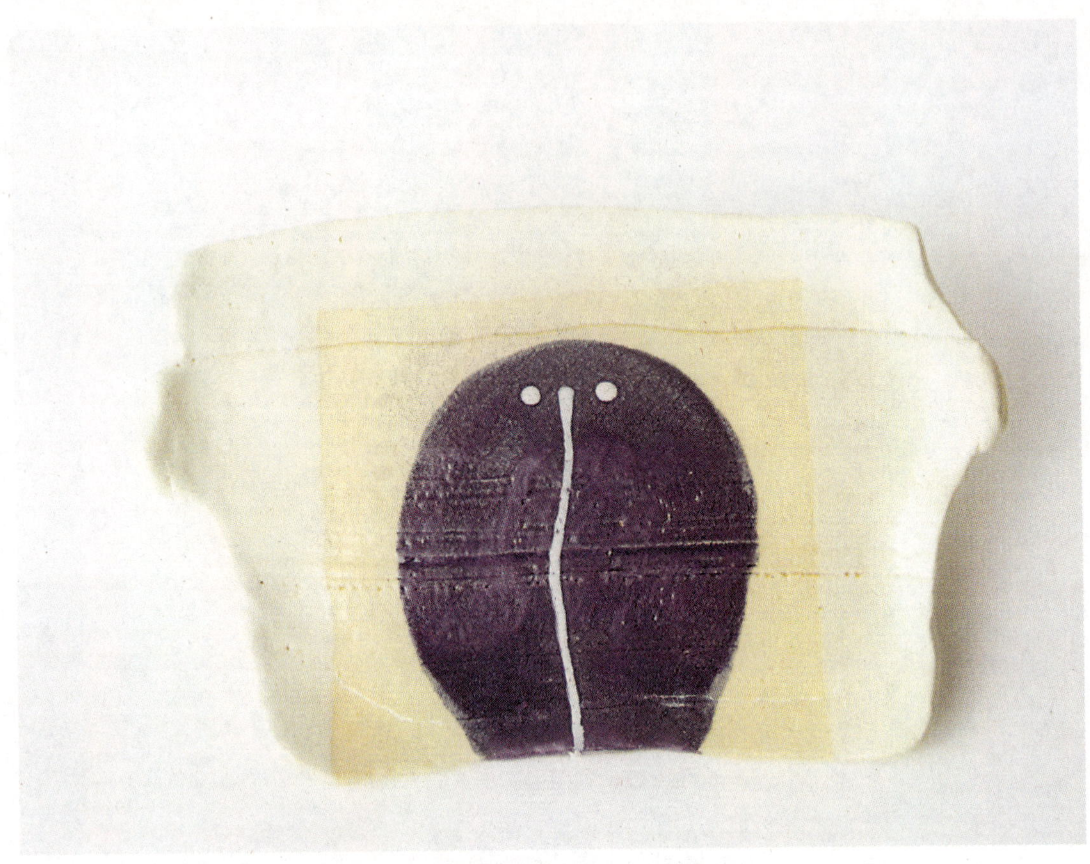

Untitled, c. 1980
Ceramic plate
6 x 9.5 inches
15.9 x 24.1 cm

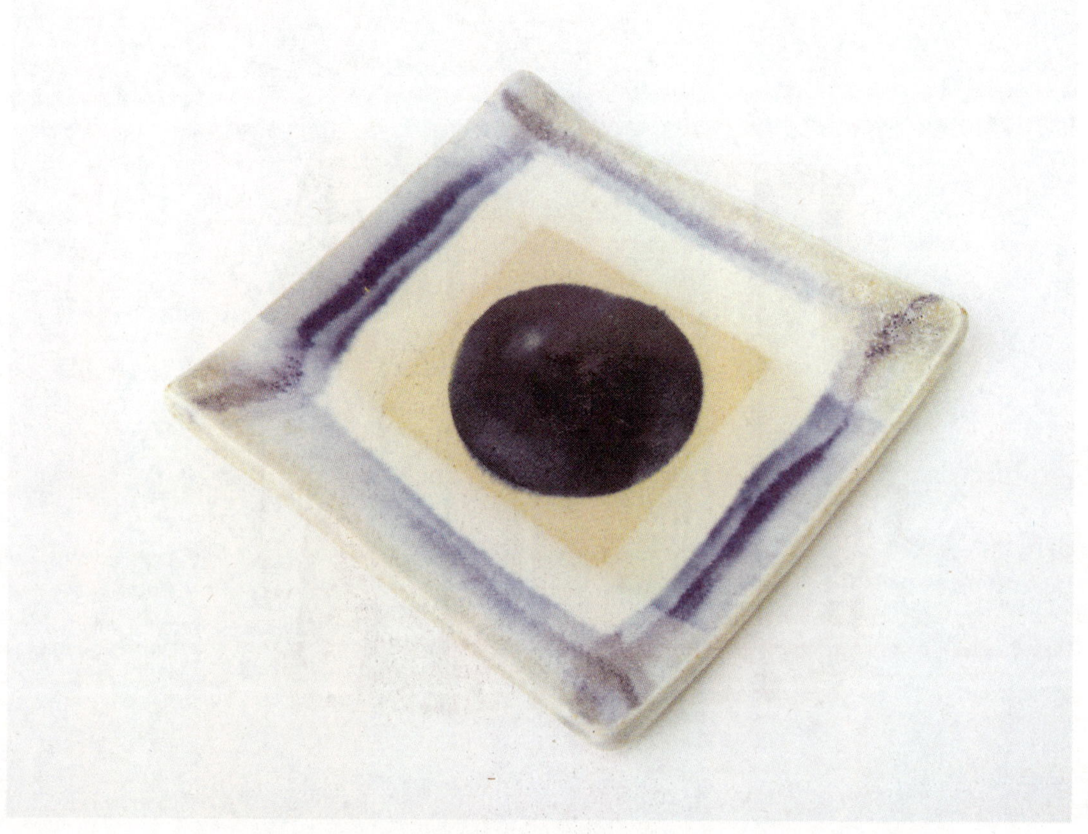

Untitled, c. 1980
Ceramic plate
7 x 7.5 inches
18.4 x 19.1 cm

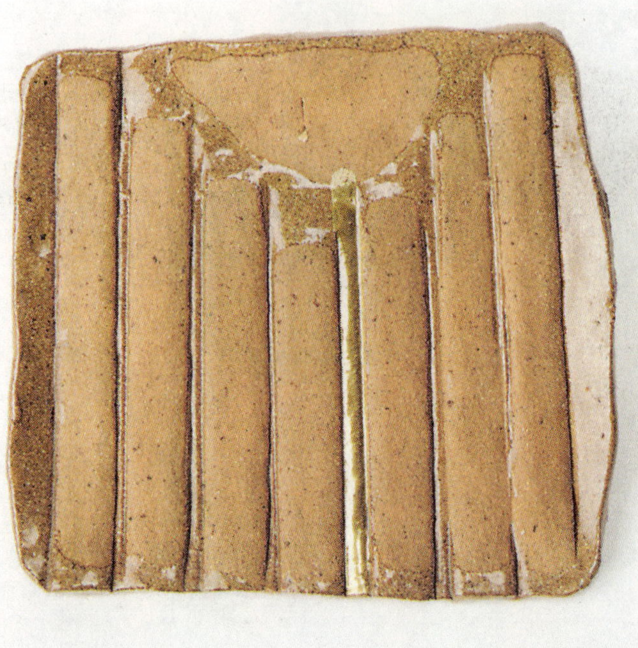

Untitled, c. 1985
Ceramic plate
6.5 x 6.5 inches
16.5 x 16.5 cm

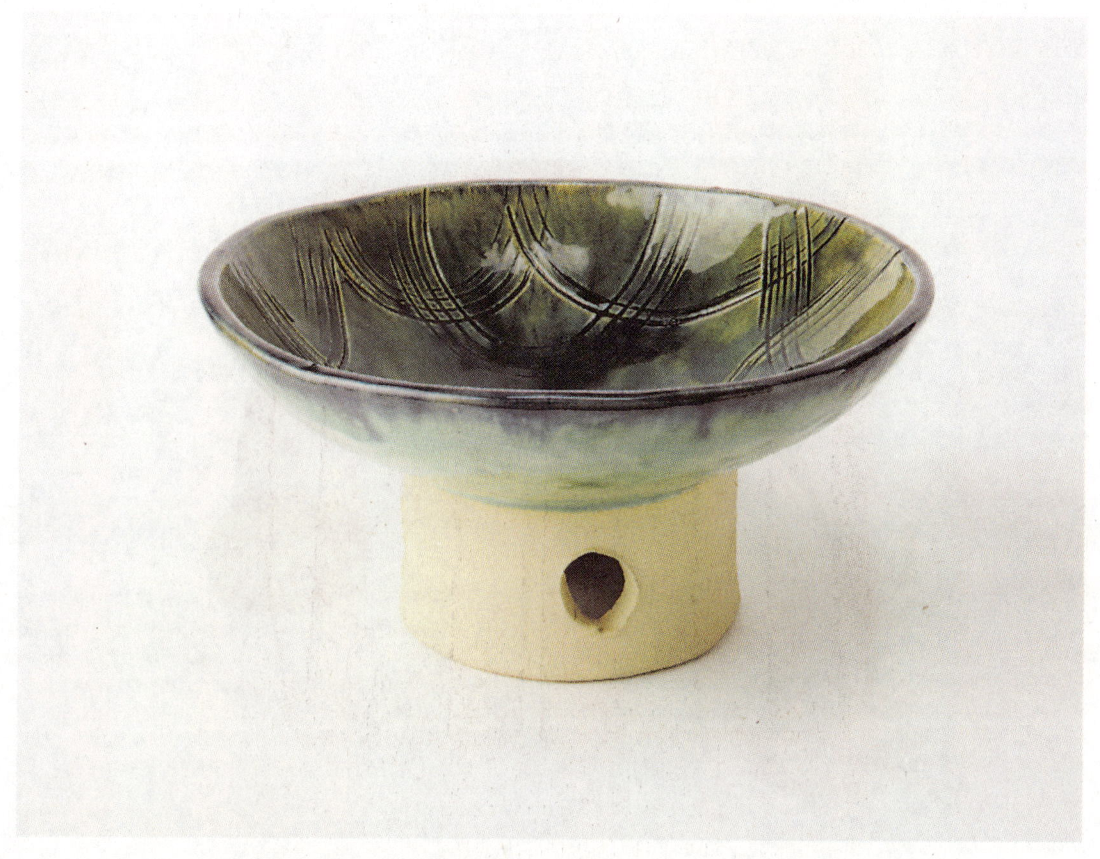

Untitled, c. 1985
Ceramic bowl
6 x 11 inches
15.2 x 27.9 cm

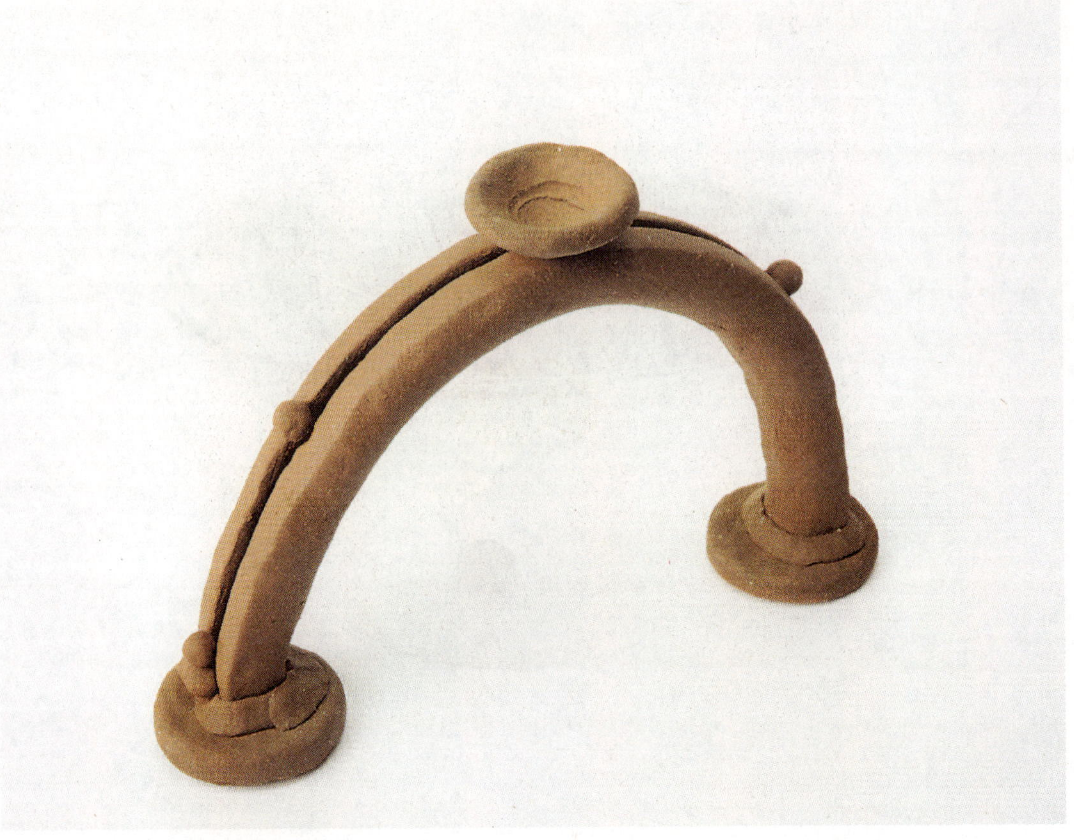

Untitled, c. 1985
Ceramic candleholder
10 x 7 inches
25.4 x 17.8 cm

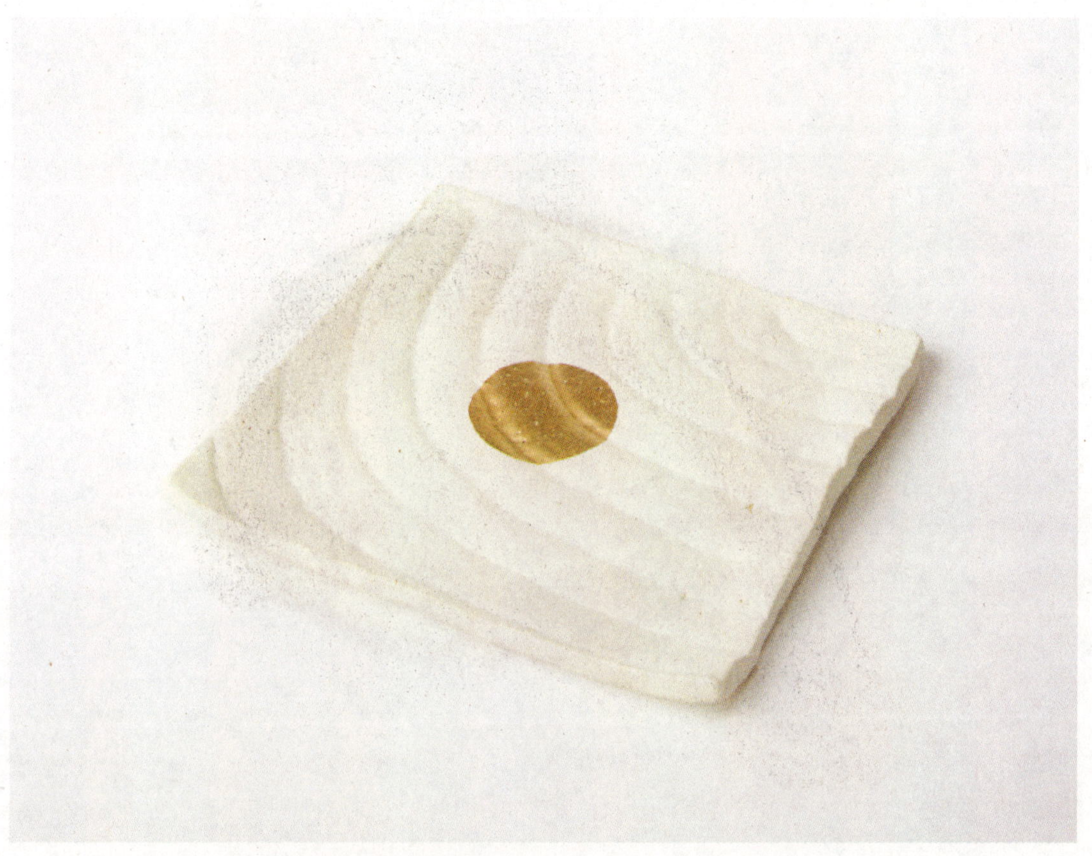

Untitled, c. 1985
Ceramic plate
7 x 7.5 inches
18.4 x 19.1 cm

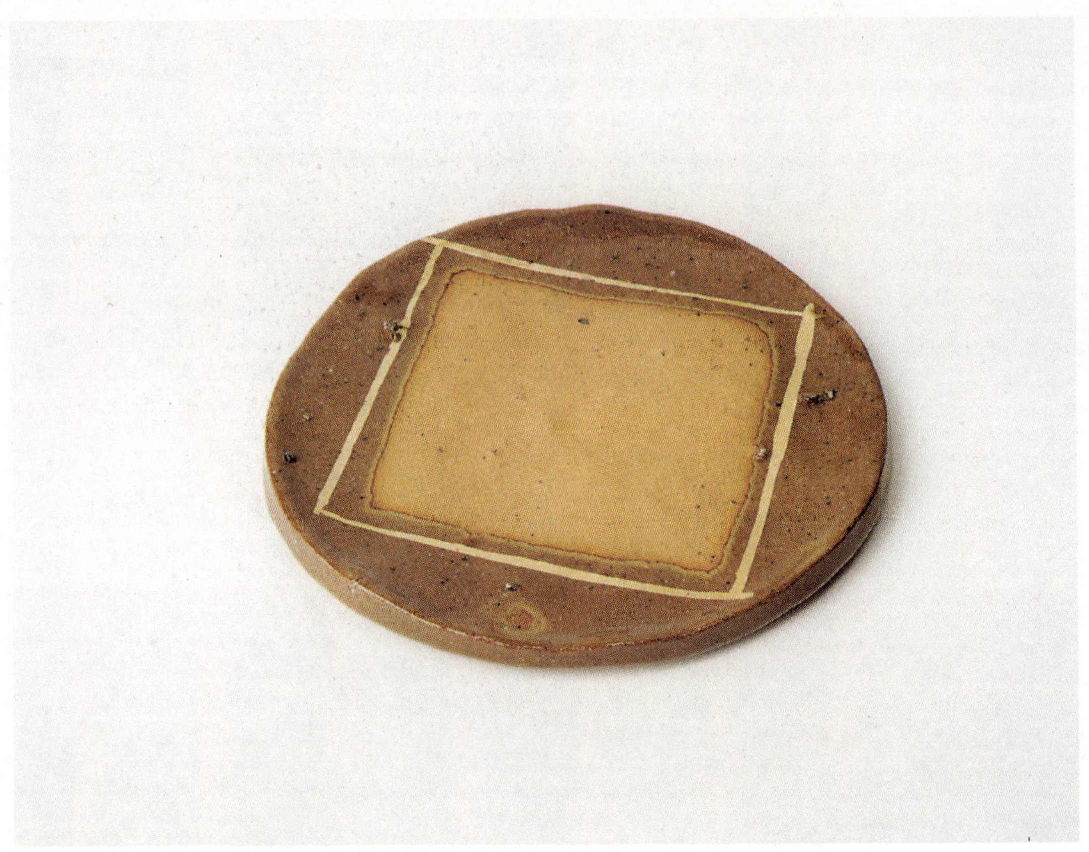

Untitled, c. 1985
Ceramic plate
7 x 7.5 inches
18.4 x 19.1 cm

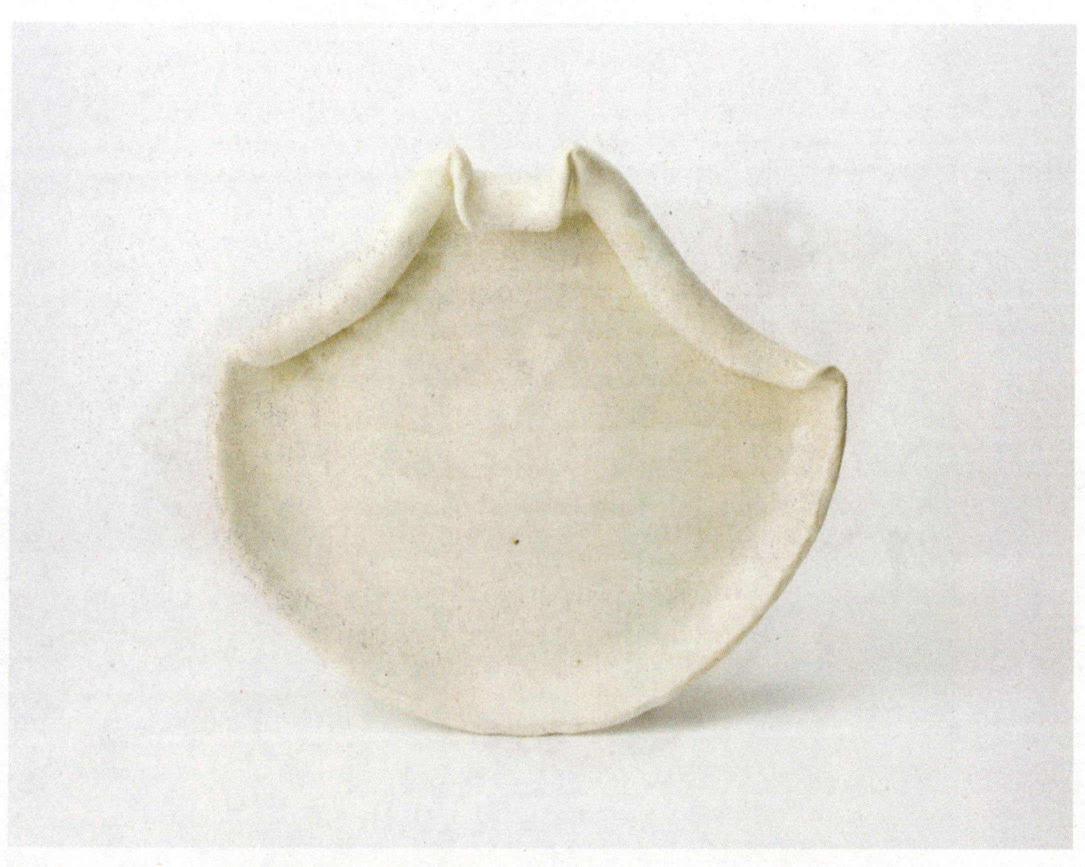

Untitled, c. 1985
Ceramic plate
12 x 10.5 inches
30.5 x 26.7 cm

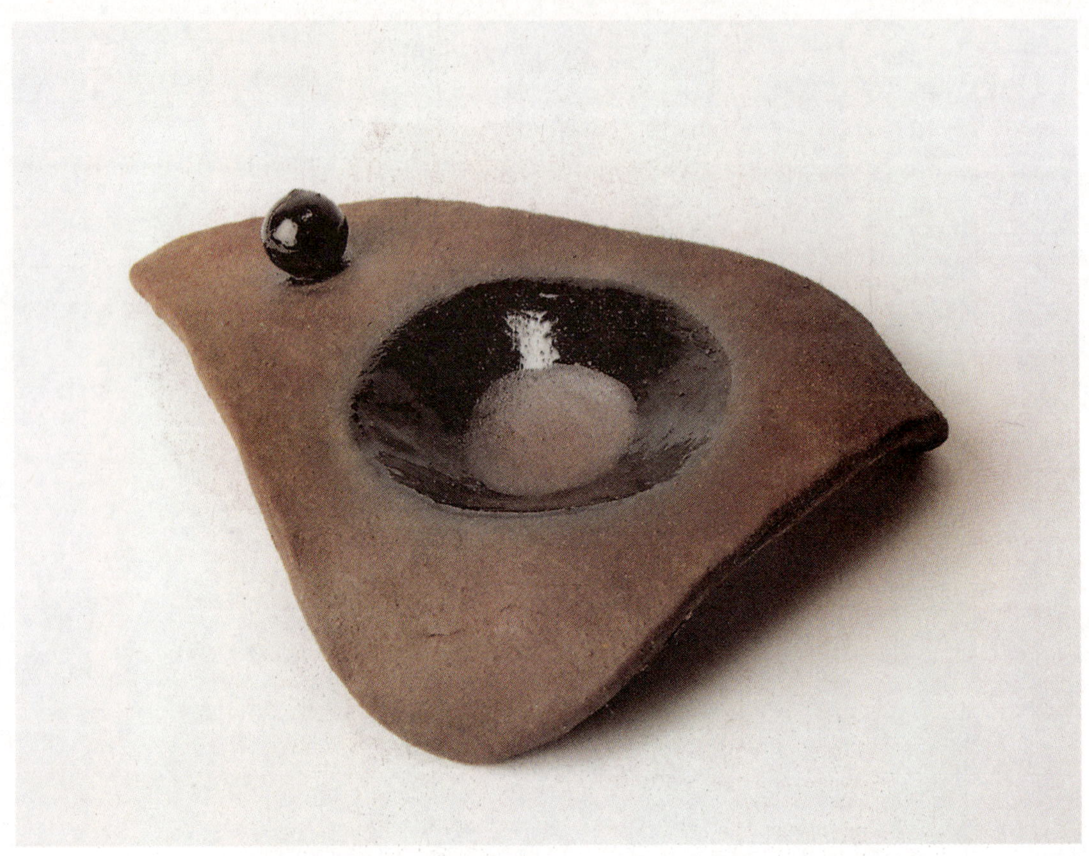

Untitled, c. 1990
Ceramic bowl
2 x 10 inches
5.1 x 25.4 cm

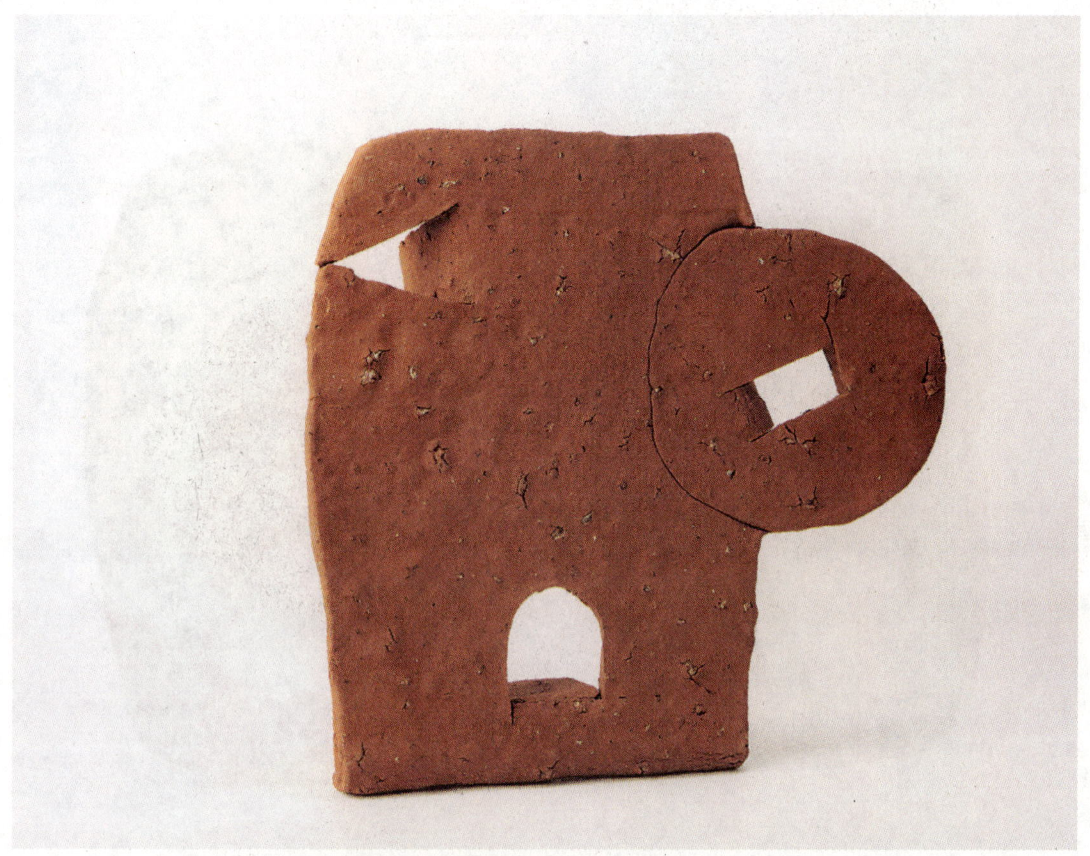

Untitled, c. 1990
Ceramic tray
14 x 15.5 x 2.5 inches
35.6 x 39.4 x 6.4 cm

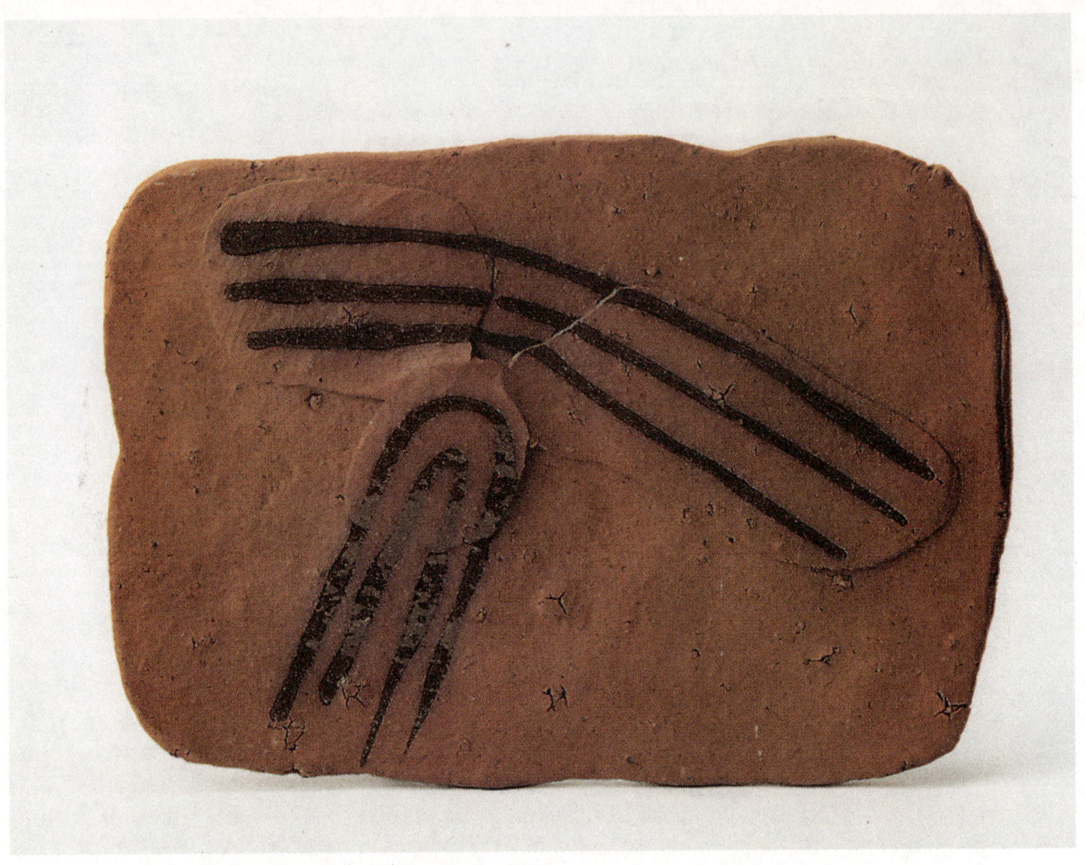

Untitled, c. 1990
Ceramic tray
13 x 9.5 inches
33 x 24.1 cm

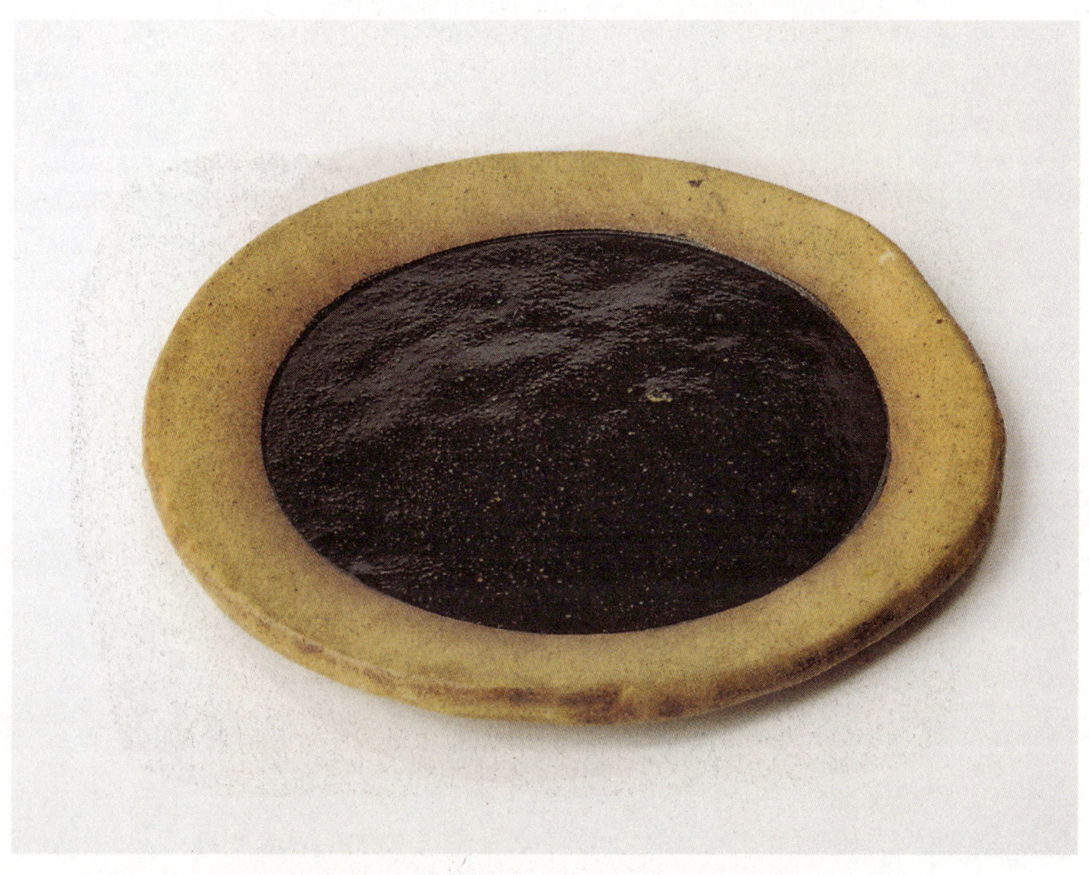

Untitled, c. 1990
Ceramic plate
9 inches
22.9 cm

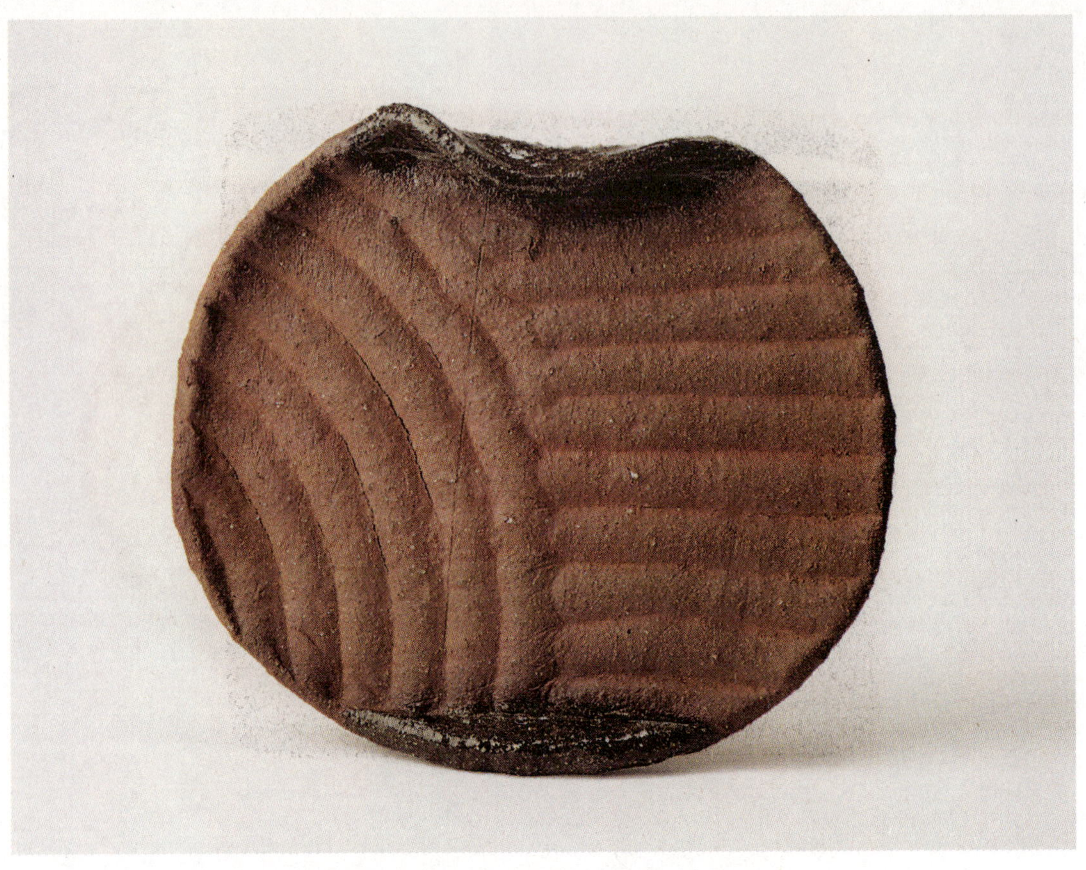

Untitled, 1979
Ceramic plate
11.5 x 10 inches
29.2 x 25.4 cm

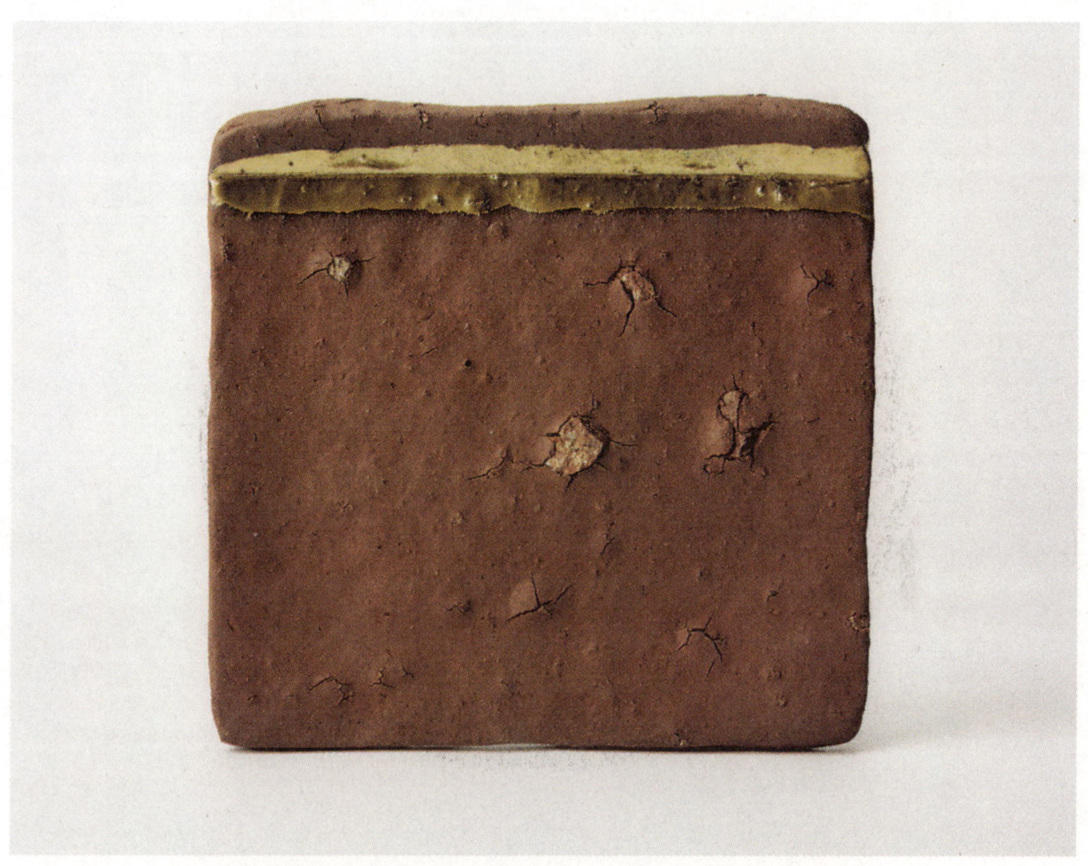

Untitled, c. 1990
Ceramic plate
9.5 x 9.5 inches
24.1 x 24.1 cm

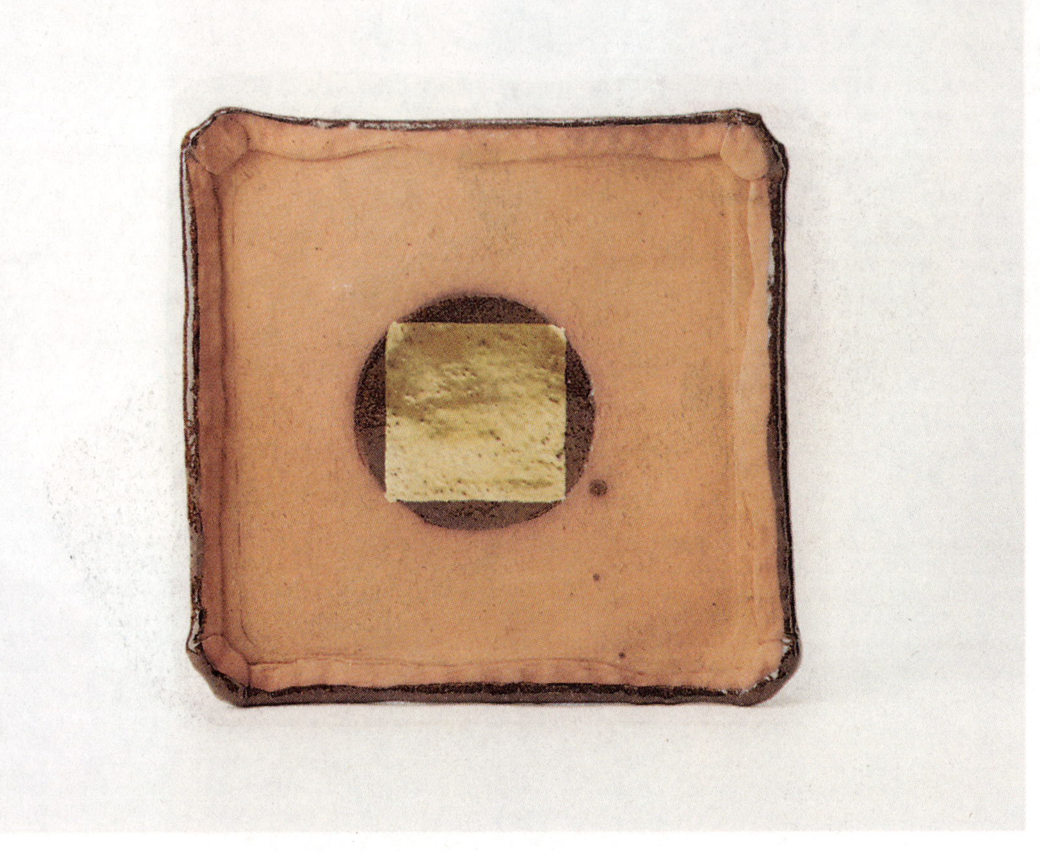

Untitled, c. 1990
Ceramic plate
12 x 12 inches
30.5 x 30.5 cm

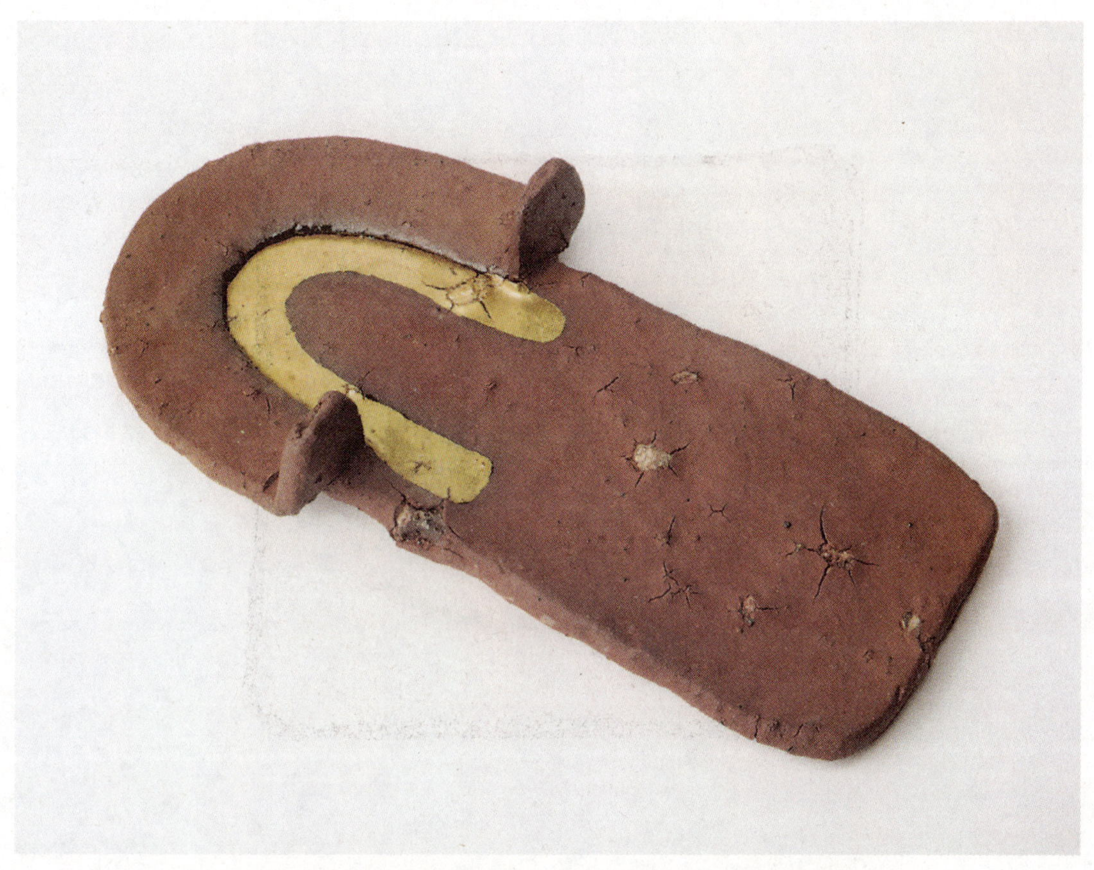

Untitled, 1992
Ceramic tray
2.5 x 17 x 8.5 inches
6.4 x 17.8 x 21.6 cm

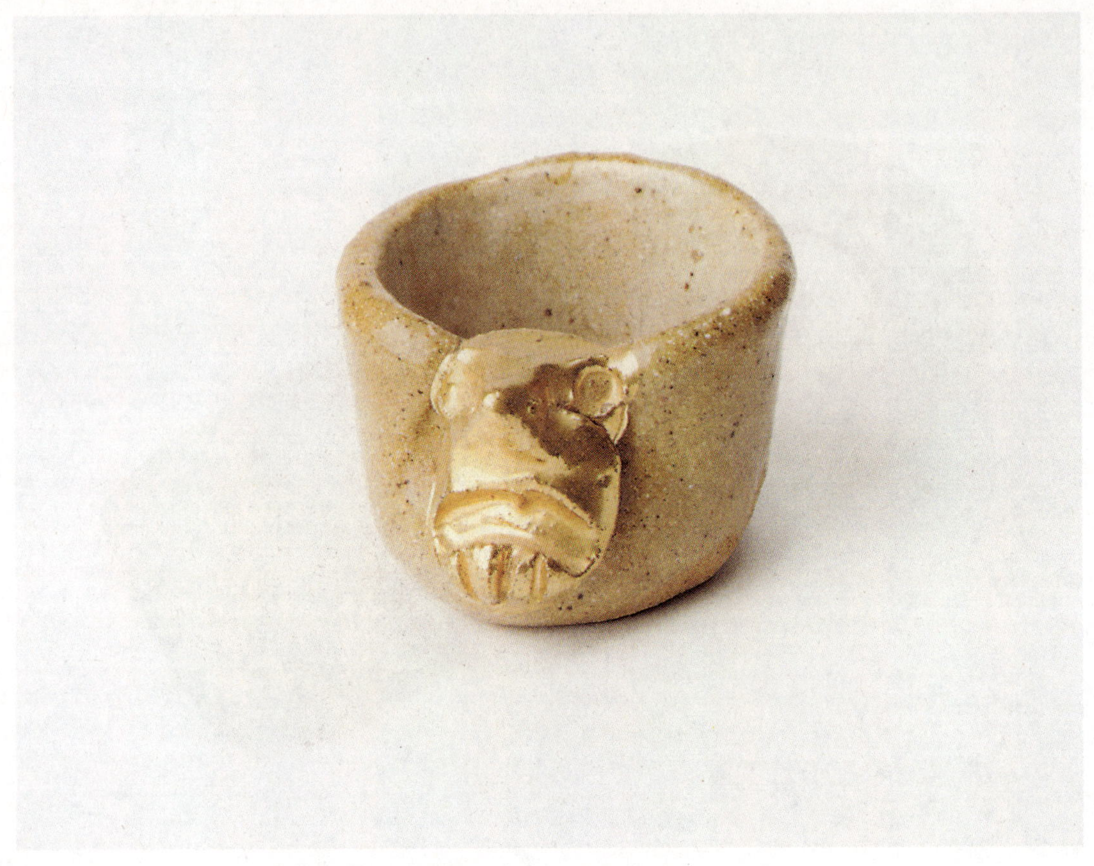

Moods of Mezcal #1/6, c. 1990
Ceramic cup
1.5 x 1.5 inches
3.8 x 3.8 cm

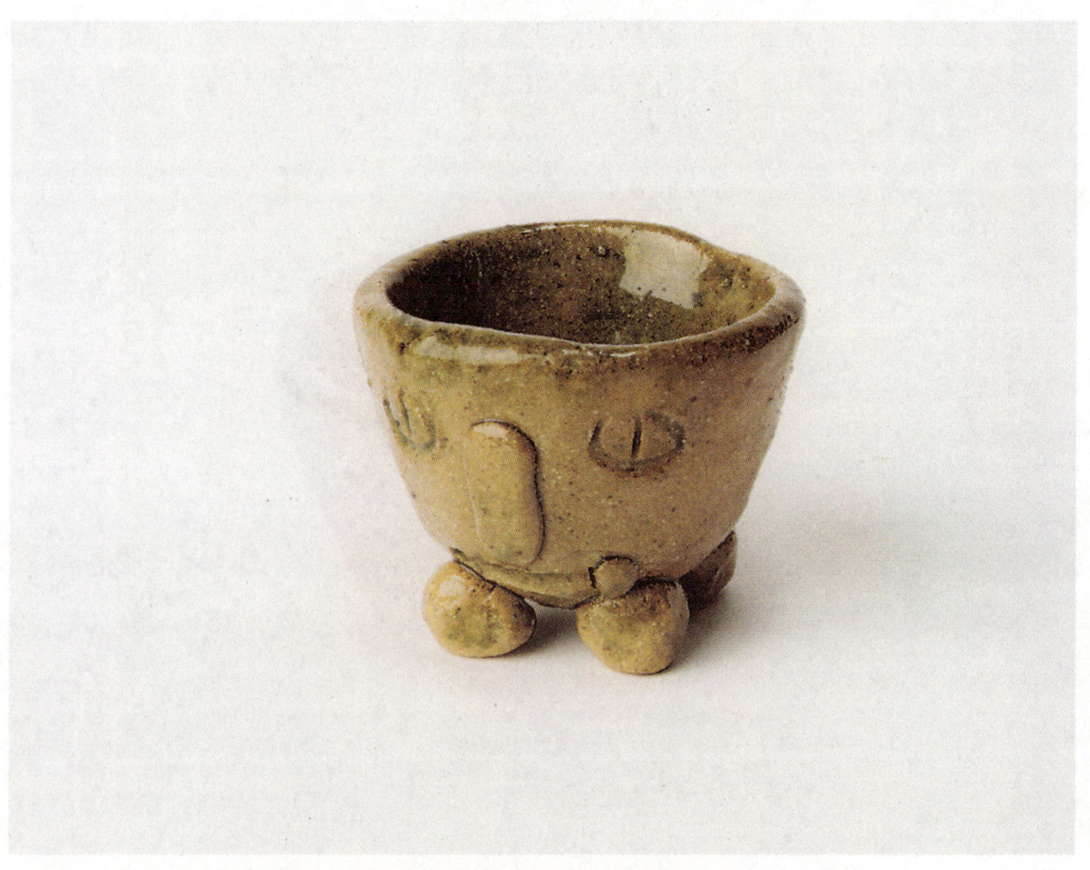

Moods of Mezcal #2/6, c. 1990
Ceramic cup
1.5 x 1.5 inches
3.8 x 3.8 cm

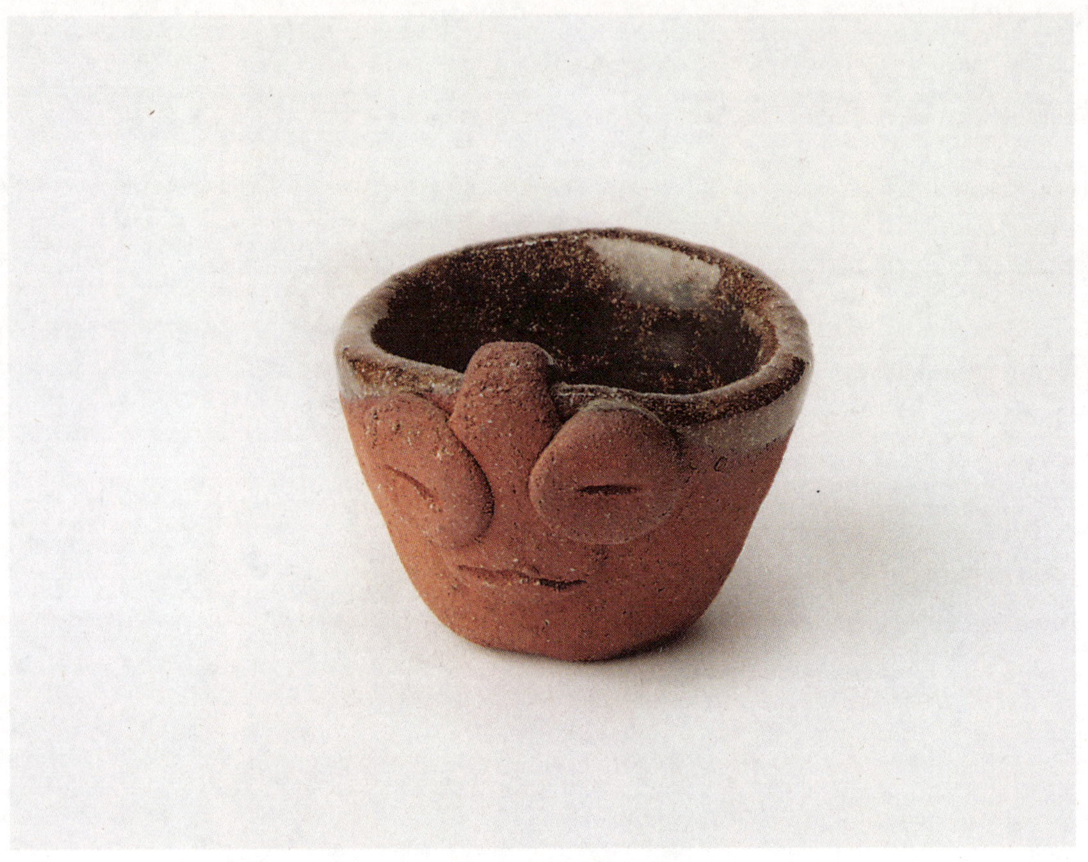

Moods of Mezcal #3/6, c. 1990
Ceramic cup
1.5 x 1.5 inches
3.8 x 3.8 cm

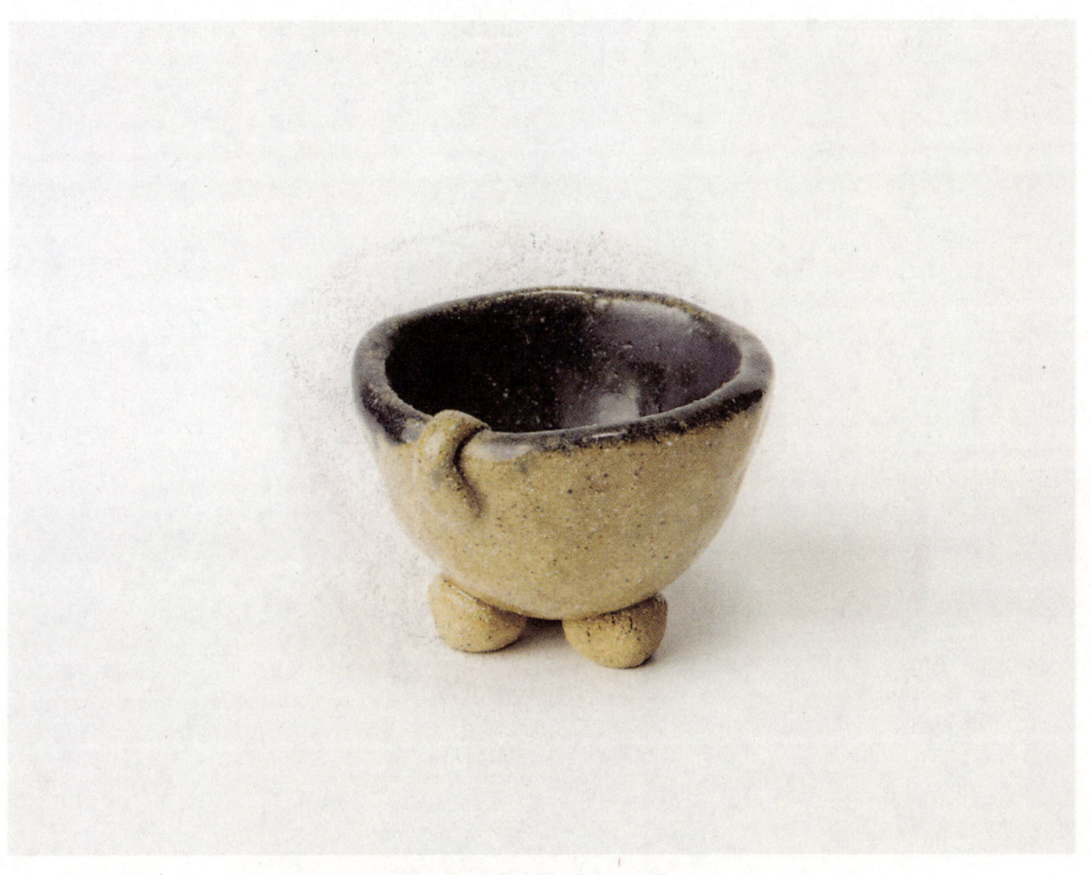

Moods of Mezcal #4/6, c. 1990
Ceramic cup
1.5 x 1.5 inches
3.8 x 3.8 cm

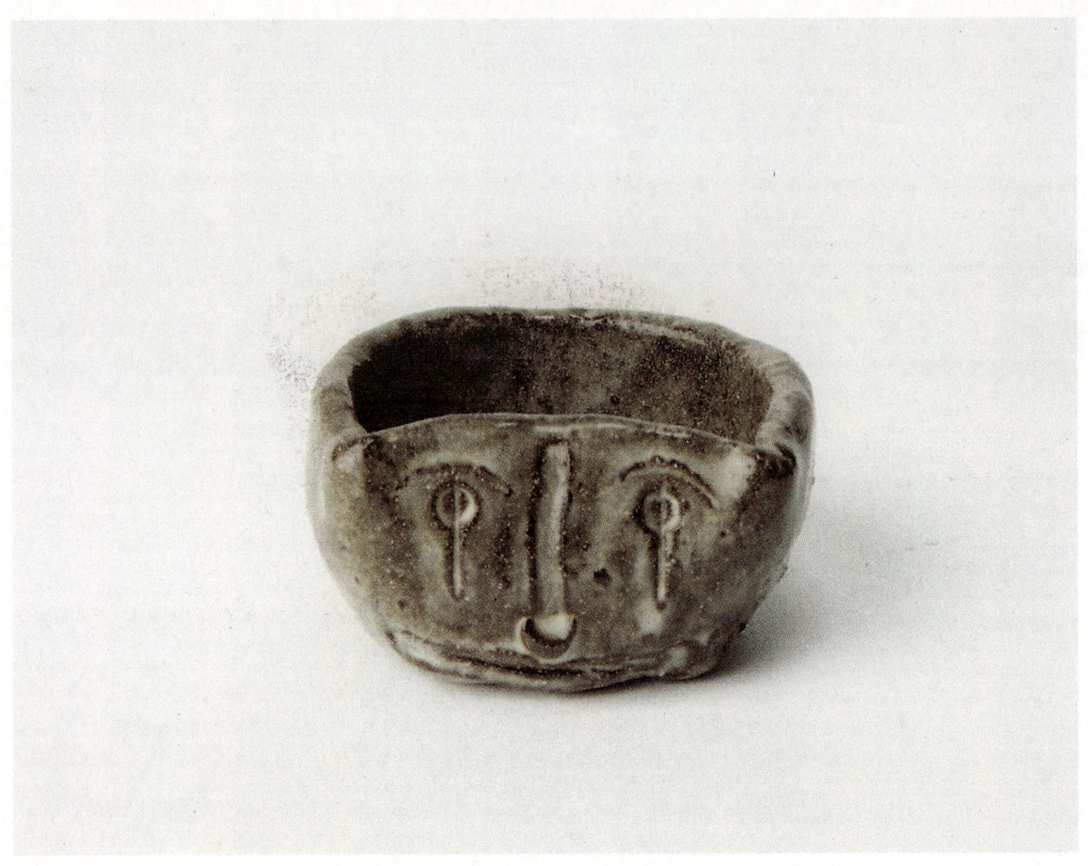

Moods of Mezcal #5/6, c. 1990
Ceramic cup
1.5 x 1.5 inches
3.8 x 3.8 cm

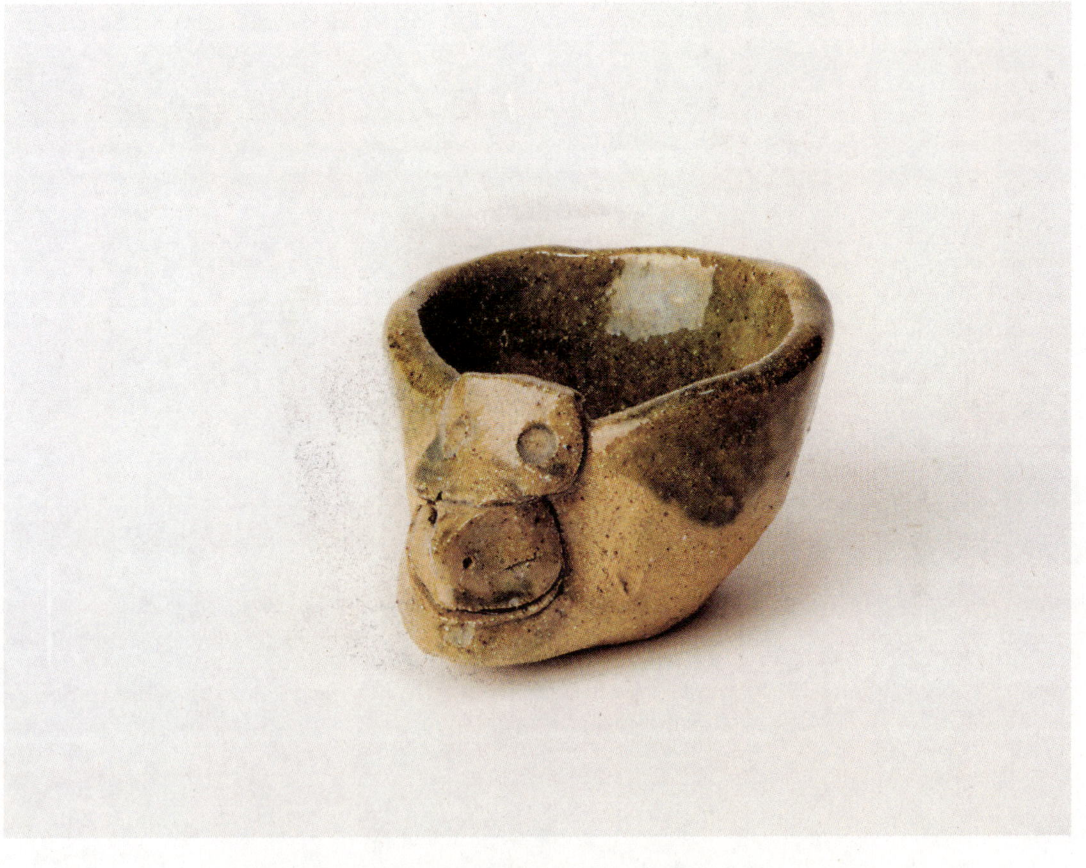

Moods of Mezcal #6/6, c. 1990
Ceramic cup
1.5 x 1.5 inches
3.8 x 3.8 cm

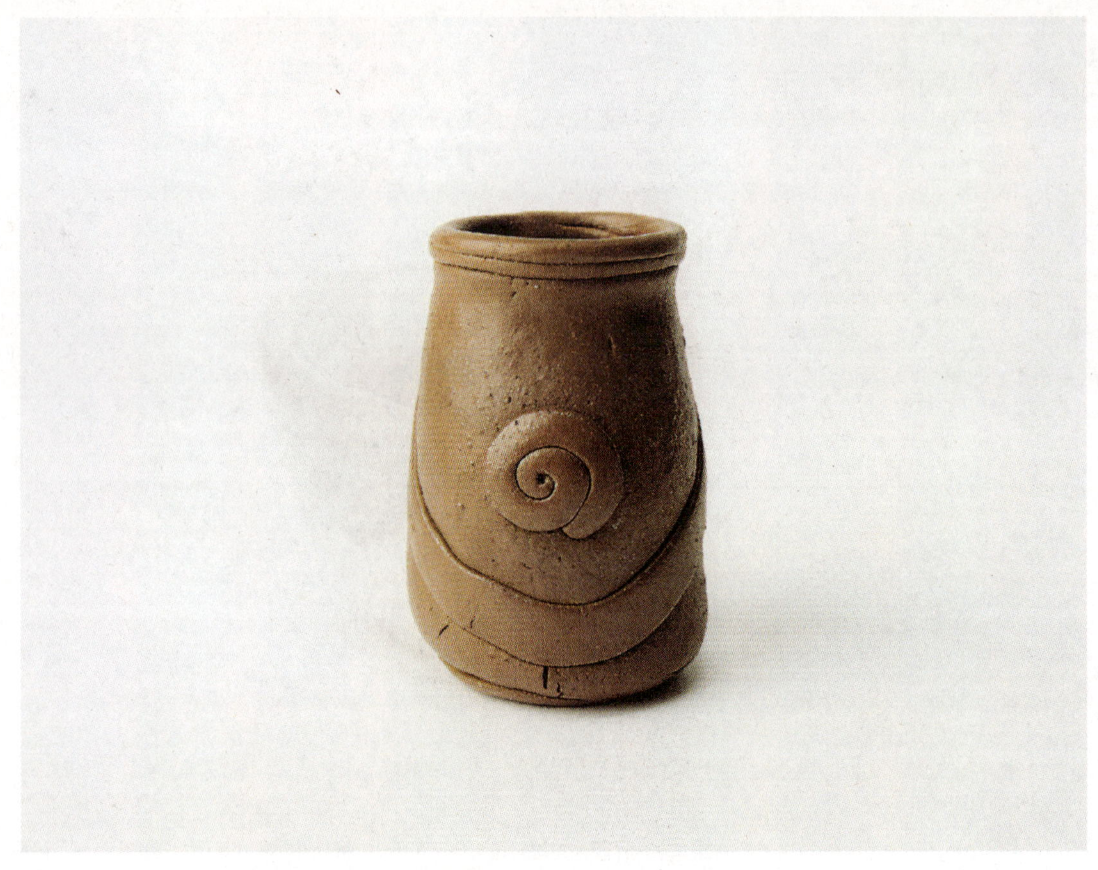

Untitled, c. 1995
Ceramic cup
4 x 2 inches
10.2 x 5 cm

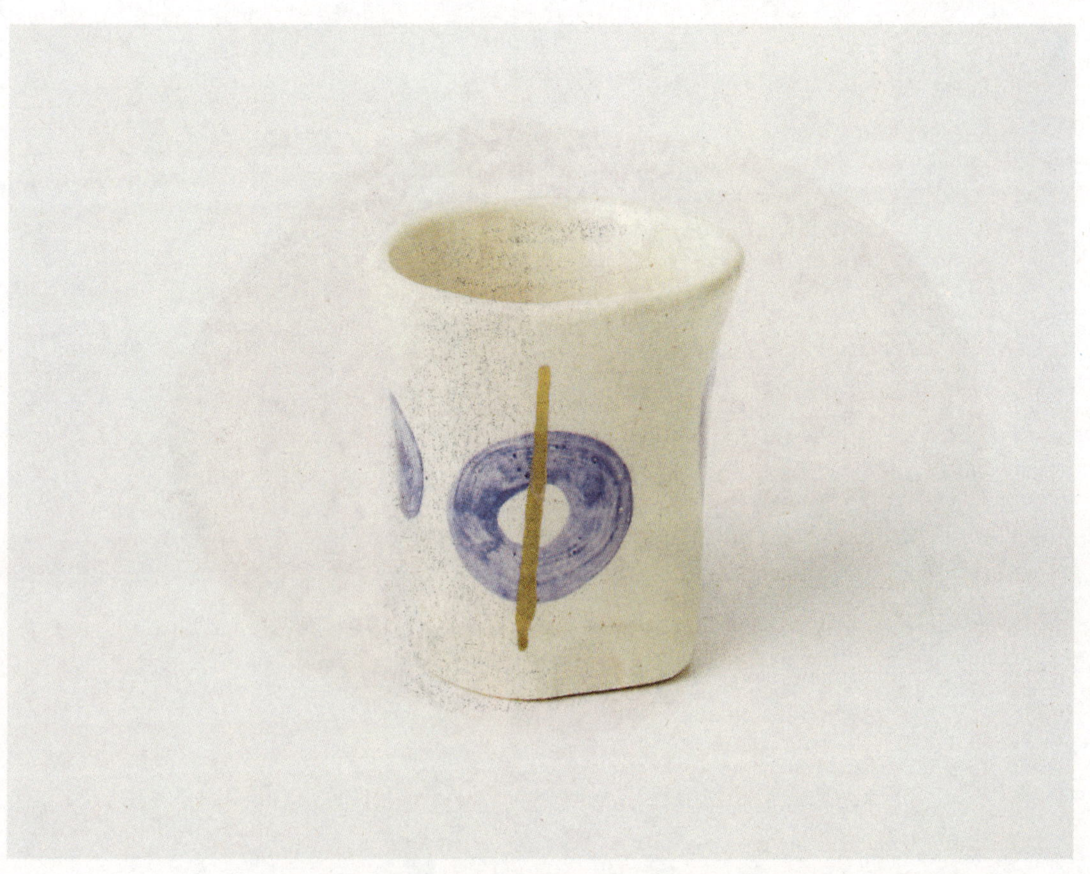

Untitled, 1999
Ceramic cup
3 x 4 inches
8.3 x 9.5 cm

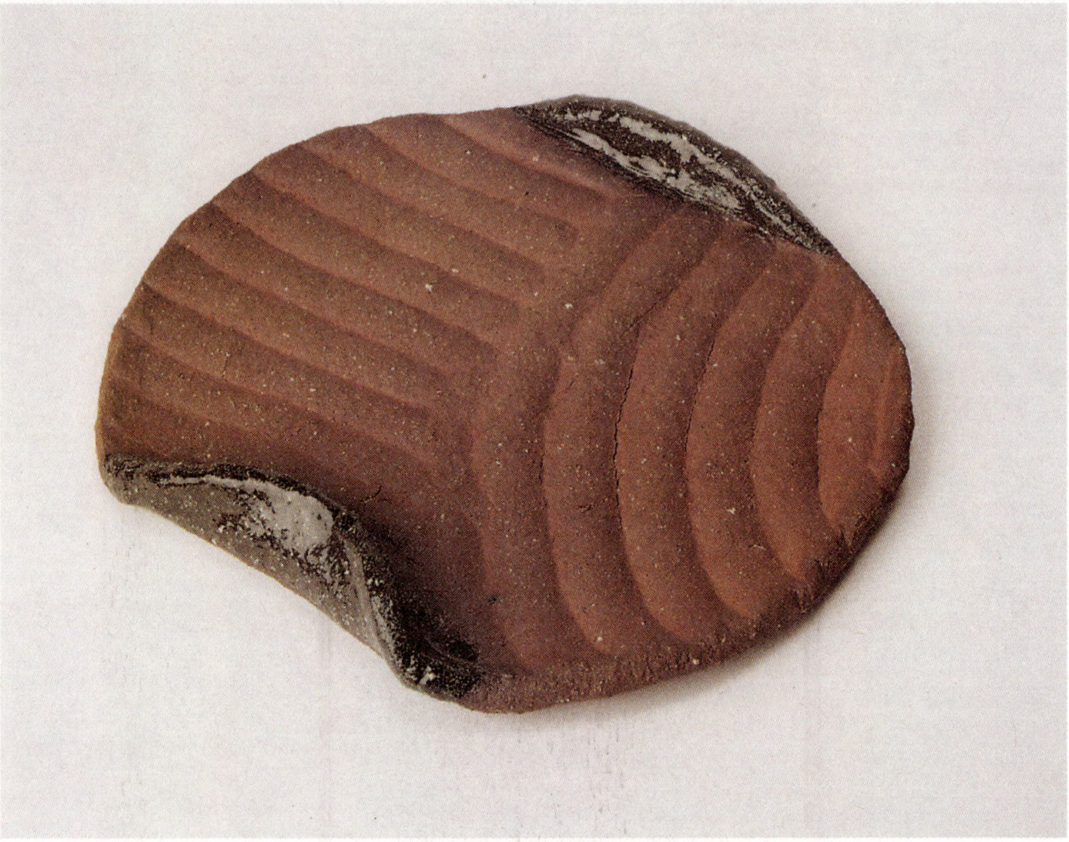

ISBN 1907908579